Dedication

With as much love as I am capable of expressing, I dedicate this book to several very special people who have loved me, endured me, and forgiven me:

To my husband, Bill, who has helped me in life and with this book more than even he realizes.

To my son, John, his wife, Marlene, and my daughter, Tracie, all of whom I thank God for giving to me.

To my father, Matt Varner, and my mother Ruby Varner, who is my idea of a real handmaiden of the Lord.

To my pastor's wife, Sister Louise Curtis, who put up with me, taught me, and never gave me cause to doubt her genuine love for Jesus.

But above all, to Jesus Himself for being my Lord and my God.

The Nitty-Gritty for Ministers' Wives

Bonnie Jean Markham

The Nitty-Gritty for Ministers' Wives

by Bonnie Jean Markham

©1988 Word Aflame Press
Hazelwood, MO 63042-2299
Reprint History: 1991, 1994, 1999, 2004

Cover Design by Tim Agnew

All Scripture quotations in this book are from the King James Version of the Bible unless otherwise identified.

All rights reserved. No portion of this publication may be reproduced, stored in an electronic system, or transmitted in any form or by any means, electronic, mechanical, photocopy, recording, or otherwise, without the prior permission of Word Aflame Press. Brief quotations may be used in literary reviews.

Printed in United States of America.

WORD AFLAME PRESS
8855 Dunn Road, Hazelwood, MO 63042
www.pentecostalpublishing.com

Library of Congress Cataloging-in-Publication Data

Markham, Bonnie Jean, 1942
The nitty-gritty for ministers' wives/Bonnie Jean Markham.
  p. cm.
ISBN 0-932581-34-X

  1. Clergymen's wives. I. Title.
BV4395.M24 1988   88-11750
253'.2—dc19   CIP

Contents

Preface 7
Chapter 1
  Face to Face with Feelings 11
Chapter 2
  Relationship with Your Husband 39
Chapter 3
  Being a Good Wife 55
Chapter 4
  Relationship with Your Children 79
Chapter 5
  Homemaking and Hospitality 105
Chapter 6
  Relationships with Members of Your Church..115
Chapter 7
  Relationships with the Former Pastor
  and Neighboring Pastors...................149
Chapter 8
  Wives of Assistant Pastors and Missionaries
  on Deputation 157
Chapter 9
  Evangelists' Wives 163
Chapter 10
  A Cloud of Witnesses 195

Preface

Titus 2:3-5 says that the older women should teach the younger, and that is the purpose of this book. My intention is to be of as much help as possible to you the minister's wife, particularly if you are young or inexperienced, and to help you realize that you are not alone in the way you feel or in the situations you face. I would like for you to sit in the kitchen with me where we can get something good to drink and have a long heart-to-heart talk. After we are comfortable I will take off my mask, and maybe by the time we are finished you will remove yours and we can become closer friends.

I have prepared for this visit for many years. Some of the things we will discuss I have learned the hard way. I have made a million mistakes but have learned through them what does not work. I have also questioned many ministers' wives who possess much more wisdom and experience than I, have observed their actions and attitudes, and have received many valuable suggestions and answers.

During two deputational tours I have had the opportunity to discuss these topics with ministers' wives in nearly every state and province of North America and with many missionary wives. These conversations have helped me to identify many problems and opportunities that we share. I sincerely appreciate the help I received from these ladies, and it is my hope that what I have gleaned will smooth out a few bumps for us all.

Thanks also goes to Sister Joan Howard of Albuquerque, New Mexico, for casting out the "demons" of bad

Preface

grammar from my original manuscript. Without her, this book would still be just a bunch of pages in my desk drawer.

Although this book focuses upon problems faced by ministers' wives, it should not be thought that their role is one big headache. The majority of the situations mentioned in this book will never happen to any one individual. While there are many difficulties and heartaches, the marvelous blessings make them worthwhile.

Any new undertaking seems almost impossible in the beginning. To a child in kindergarten even the alphabet may seem overwhelming. From our youth we all have to learn to accomplish our tasks one at a time, and with the help of the Lord, I am sure we can handle anything we may have to face. It is really our very own attitude that will make our being a minister's wife a drudgery or a delight. As for me—I love it!

The truth is that being chosen by the Lord to be the helpmate of a man of God is one of the greatest privileges and honors on earth. The King of the universe has already chosen you to be His bride—the Prince of Peace wants you to be His helpmate. Now the everlasting Father has placed you in the position of caring for His children. What trust Jesus has in you! What confidence! And all you need to accomplish your task, besides the Holy Ghost, is a willingness to learn, a clean and sincere heart, patience, and lots of elbow grease.

As you read, bear in mind that there is no way anyone could give ironclad, perfect answers to many of the following questions. Life itself is too diverse and people too varied. Situations are colored by thousands of individual experiences. A perfect response in one instance could be deadly in another. Treat two people alike and one may love you and the other despise you. One pastor's wife may use a method with outstanding results, but another wife using the same method, in an attempt to be like her, may cause a church split.

With this in mind, I offer the following suggestions only as guidelines—not as cut and dried, cure-all answers. The responses given are answers that have worked the majority of times—not every time. You must carefully and prayerfully consider your husband's personality (and is there anyone just like him?), his call, his goals, and even his hang-ups. Consider your own personality, your own children, and your own congregation. The size of your church must be considered in many situations as well as your members' personalities and even their length of time in church.

Above all, you must please Jesus Christ. That is your first priority. You won't even please your husband all the time, much less all your members, but if you keep your heart, attitude, and spirit right in the sight of God, then you will be all He intends for you to be and you will please Him. When you get discouraged, remember that Jesus is more than worth all the problems you may face. Learn to accept your responsibilities by bearing in mind at all times that you are doing these things for Him and that He will reward you far beyond the cost to you in time and effort.

The Lord asks us to do more than what man requires when He says to go the second mile for others. Surely, then, He is even more pleased when we willingly go the second mile for Him. Let's really make an effort to please Him; let's do our best to accomplish more than just what

Preface

is required.

Your goal should never be merely to become or do what people expect you to be or do, or you will tear your hair out (or maybe theirs). Your goal must forever be to please your Savior, and if you do this, you will please the majority of your members as well and live a full, exciting, and satisfying life.

Bear in mind also that He created you as you are, and if you will make an honest effort, He will take the responsibility for your results and also for what may seem to be a *lack* of results. When you try your very best and still seem to be woefully lacking in results, remember that you are called according to *His* purpose—not yours. Many times the people who accomplish things for God never realize the important part they play in the lives of others. So don't be concerned about man's ideas of success and don't strive for popularity and recognition, but rather be concerned with what the Lord considers greatness: "If any man desire to be first, the same shall be last of all, and servant of all" (Mark 9:35). "Whosoever will be great among you, let him be your minister; And whosoever will be chief among you, let him be your servant: Even as the Son of man came not to be ministered unto, but to minister" (Matthew 20:26-28).

The purpose of this book, then, is to help you learn how to *serve* and how to *give* in order to be a blessing to others. In the process, you will receive God's choicest blessings in return.

May this book help you both to *receive* God's blessing and to *be* a blessing. "I will bless thee . . . and thou shalt be a blessing" (Genesis 12:2).

Chapter One

Face to Face with Feelings

None of us is alike on the inside anymore than we are alike on the outside. We are not all beautiful (unfortunately). Neither are we all musically talented or gifted in crafts and clever ideas for Sunday school.

Contrary to many young wives' fears, a woman does not have to know how to play a musical instrument or "sing like a bird" to be a good minister's wife. It is indeed helpful and a real blessing, but it is not a requirement. Neither Sister Catherine Chambers, the wife of our former general superintendent, Sister Judy Maki, who has evangelized with her husband for many years in the States and in many foreign countries, nor I can sing or play any instruments; but so far the Lord has managed to bless our husbands' ministries without any musical contribution on our part.

Please don't torment yourself if you are not musically gifted. The Giver of all gifts knew your capabilities when He called you. It is far more important to love people than to dazzle them with talents.

Although we are not all alike physically, we do share common physical features such as two eyes, one nose, one mouth, and so on. Likewise we share similarities on the inside as well. We all have doubts, fears, failures, hang-ups, weaknesses, strengths and successes. It is only our particular combination of these characteristics that makes us unique. No one has invented a new emotion since God created man, so we must not think that we are alone in the way we feel.

Don't compare yourself with others. There will always be some better and some worse; just do your best, accept yourself, and let the Potter mold you into a vessel that pleases Him. Just being and acting yourself will relieve a lot of pressure.

None of us on earth always knows exactly what to do in every situation, lives up to our best intentions, or is as spiritual as we would like to be. We all have good days full of victory and faith when we feel that we are a fine person, and then we have our days of discouragement and disappointment when we feel that we are anything *but* a fine person. For the most part we are somewhere in between. Our days run together with our own particular routine even if that routine is hectic.

The Bible recommends moderation in all things. Too many peaks and valleys too close together are not healthy, so be content with your own particular routine. There will be days when you feel that you have the most wonderful people in all the world and other days when you feel that you could cheerfully blow up the church with all the people in it—including your husband. But don't worry, you are normal. Just ask the Lord to hide the dynamite until things take a turn for the better.

Face to Face with Feelings

It is very important that we understand a few things about emotions, for human beings are emotional creatures and that we cannot ignore. We must admit that our emotions are not all happy ones, and to expect for us or the members of our churches to be always on the mountaintop is unrealistic. We must realize that everyone's life is made up of sad times as well as glad times, and we must learn to cope with the varied circumstances of life. According to Ecclesiastes 3, there is a season (a season consists of *many* days) and a time for every purpose under heaven. There is a time

To be born	To die
To plant	To pluck up that which is planted
To heal	To kill
To build up	To break down
To laugh	To weep
To dance	To mourn
To gather stones together	To cast away stones
To embrace	To refrain from embracing
To get	To lose
To keep	To cast away
To sew	To rend
To speak	To keep silence
To love	To hate
Of peace	Of war

What smooth sailing we could have through life if we could just stay in the left-hand column and stay out of those times indicated on the right! But God has a purpose for those times as well. We must learn to trust Him when we are in the middle of an uncomfortable season.

Your life, my life, and the lives of the members of our churches will be drawn from both columns, so do not criticize yourself if you do not bubble over with cheerfulness at all hours of the day and night. Likewise have patience and longsuffering when someone in your church goes through a trying time. Not only should you laugh with those who laugh, but you should also cry with those who cry. Be thankful that, even when circumstances bring chaos into your life, you can still have peace, knowing that all is well with your soul and that Jesus will bring you through even the roughest of storms.

Trials and Suffering

Some people deny that suffering exists for true Christians, while others seem to wallow in it. Some wear their suffering on their sleeve for the whole world to see. They are forever sad and gloomy and can speak of nothing but the trials, heartaches, and misery that they suffer because they are so devout. Their speech and attitude seem to state, "Pity me; I am a Christian." On the other hand, I have heard and read that if a person is a sincere, dedicated Christian, his life will be a continual bowl of cherries with nothing but blessings, joy, cheerfulness, health, and prosperity stretching from here to the farthest horizon, and that if his life is not bubbly and enthusiastic, then he has no faith and something is drastically wrong between him and God.

One precious minister's wife became very ill while doing her best to serve God. Searching her heart and conscience, she repented of anything and everything that even might be the cause. Although she felt completely right with God, and in spite of being prayed for countless times, she did not receive healing. One day she listened to a message on tape that said, "If you are sick or suffering, it is because you have sin in your life, and you need to repent." The poor lady became nearly hysterical and was inconsolable for some time. She could not imagine why God was punishing her so severely for something and not telling her what it was so that she could make it right. Of course, we should examine ourselves for unrepented sins and sinful attitudes that may be a factor in some cases, but they certainly are not always the cause of sickness and problems.

Let us search the Scriptures to see if genuine children of God ever experience distressing situations.

Noah found grace in the eyes of the Lord and obeyed Him completely, but he still had to endure the pain of seeing his whole world destroyed and all his family, friends, and neighbors die except for his immediate family. I cannot picture Noah standing at the window grinning when all of this took place. It was, no doubt, an exceptionally painful experience that few people could have endured. Except for the grace that Noah received, he and his family could not have borne it either.

The Israelites were slaves to the Egyptians for four hundred years and suffered terrible atrocities. According to Hebrews 11:25, Moses chose to suffer afflictions with the people of God. Afflictions hurt!

According to Hebrews 11:35-38, God's people at various times were tortured (which is hard for the best Christian to experience with enthusiasm) and endured cruel mockings, scourgings, bonds, and imprisonment. They were stoned, sawn asunder, tempted, and slain with the sword; they wandered in sheepskins and goatskins; they were desperate, destitute (no prosperity there), afflicted, and tormented; they wandered in deserts, mountains, dens and caves. In one word, they *suffered.* Did these trials come because of sins they committed? No! Hebrews 11:38 says the world was not worthy of them.

Job's "comforters" told him time and again that he was a sinner in need of repentance, or else he would be enjoying God's blessings instead of undergoing so much pain, sorrow, and sickness. Yet God had pointed him out to Satan and said, "There is none like him in the earth, a perfect and an upright man, one that feareth God, and escheweth evil" (Job 1:8). While God Himself did not consider Job sinful, He still allowed him to suffer, and through suffering Job learned a great many things, including much about himself and about God.

The early Christians probably did not enjoy being thrown to the lions. Even Jesus spent the night before Calvary agonizing in prayer because of the suffering involved in bearing our sins on the cross. Hebrews 2:10 says that the captain of our salvation was made perfect through suffering.

Many people unconsciously consider only the North American church, but actually the bride of Christ is found in other countries as well, and in many lands she suffers cruel opposition even today.

Clearly, then, it is possible for a genuine, consecrated child of God to suffer. Such a person should not be made to feel guilty when she finds herself in sickness or in extremely painful situations. However, she should be encouraged to endure her situation with as few complaints as possible instead of acting as if her suffering was proof of her righteousness.

Neither sickness and suffering nor health and prosperity are gauges that we can use to determine if a person is a saint or a sinner. Proverbs 13:15 tells us, "The way of transgressors is hard," while Psalm 34:19 says, "Many are the afflictions of the righteous." In other words saints and sinners alike are subject to problems. The child of God definitely has the advantage, however, because Psalm 34:19 goes on to say, ". . . but the LORD delivereth him out of them all." Moreover, our hope is not in this life only but in the one to come.

Hearing people continually complain of their problems, sicknesses, and heartaches is very depressing, and voicing such complaints is no way to win others to the Lord. We should, therefore, teach our people to worship, praise, and exalt Jesus to such a degree that people who come to our church services will be uplifted, inspired, edified, and encouraged. Everybody already knows that the world is full of problems, but a church service is not the time to discuss everyone's personal problems. They can be handled in confidential counseling sessions but should not be discussed during public testimony services. For members to come week after week and hear about how hard things are and how sinful the world is will eventually pull them down. God inhabits the praises of His people, so if we truly want His presence and power in our services, they should be full of praise and thanksgiving, not public discussion of problems.

Although we do have problems, God allows them to come for our good in the long run. We should learn to give thanks for the way God uses problems in our lives. I Peter 5:10 states, "But the God of all grace, who hath called us unto his eternal glory by Christ Jesus, after that ye have suffered a while, make you perfect, stablish, strengthen, settle you." We are not expected to enjoy the problem, but we should be thankful for the purpose, whatever it may be, that God has in allowing us to face it.

Isaiah 26:3 promises, "Thou wilt keep him in perfect peace, whose mind is stayed on thee: because he trusteth in thee." Philippians 4:6 admonishes, "Be careful [anxious] for nothing; but in every thing by prayer and supplication with thanksgiving let your requests be made known unto God." Do these verses mean that we should never feel concern but be happy and glad even when a loved one is diagnosed as having incurable cancer, when a teenager runs away from home and cannot be found, when a man with a family loses his job, when a spouse is unfaithful, or when a little child contracts a serious disease that could leave him mentally or physically handicapped for life? Does Philippians 4:6 mean we should not give problems a thought, not care, not do anything about them, ignore them, and let the chips fall where they may?

I hardly think so. Times such as these are fiery trials, and anyone who experiences them would be very much aware of the heat and pain and would give a great deal of thought as to the best way to quench the flames. When a house catches on fire we do not sit calmly in our easy chairs and ask God to send a few buckets of water, but we jump up and find buckets and water hoses. If need be we send for men who are trained to put out fires. Likewise, when we have other types of problems, we should do whatever we are able to do, which means we will have to give these matters much thought, prayer, fasting and physical action, while asking God for help and guidance.

Face to Face with Feelings

The man who loses his job cannot just retire until people come beating on his door to give him another one. Sometimes God sends a job very quickly, but usually the man must think, plan, and look for one. Everything possible should be done for the cancer victim and the stricken child, but unless God heals instantaneously, these situations will involve a great deal of thought as to the proper decisions to make, seeking the will of God and the best possible course of action.

Do your utmost to find the runaway teen, and get official help if it is needed. Do your best to save a troubled marriage. Do what you can and should to solve any other problem that may come your way, but while you are doing everything humanly possible, let your mind and soul find peace in the midst of the storm by keeping your mind stayed on the Lord and trusting Jesus to do what you cannot do. Don't worry and fret about the situation. As you fervently pray for help and guidance, give God glory by thanking Him.

Just as Jesus prayed that if it were possible He wanted the cup to pass from Him, we also prefer to be spared our time of agony. We do not thank God for a problem in the sense that we are glad to have it, but rather we thank Him for the purpose that He has in allowing it to try us. He has promised that, in spite of the pain, we will be improved by the very thing that seems about to destroy us and that all things will work together for our good (Romans 8:28), but we must keep the right spirit and attitude in order for His purpose to be fulfilled.

While we should never question God's mercy, love, or wisdom in allowing something to happen, it is in order to ask Him to help us understand the reason certain things must be as they are. There is a vast difference between questioning God and asking God questions.

Sometimes the Lord may give us a test in order to move us to a higher spiritual grade level. However, some people never move up because they never pass the test for their current level. They murmur, complain, and blame others; some become bitter and backslide. But in time, those who bear trials and testing as things God has allowed for a good purpose and who keep a good spirit in spite of the pain and tears invariably move to higher, happier planes in God.

There is a great difference between counseling with close friends to draw comfort from discussing problems with them and complaining to anyone who will listen. Everyone needs someone to help them at times, but complaining never does any good.

After Jesus prayed to have the cup pass from Him, He then added, "Nevertheless not as I will, but as thou wilt" (Matthew 26:39). He then went on to face betrayal by those He loved, mocking from the public, scourging, and crucifixion by those He had created to love Him. He didn't like the suffering and would have liked to have it pass from Him, but He endured it for us. Likewise, we are not expected to *enjoy* our times of suffering but to *endure* them with a heart full of trust and love for God and a thankfulness for His power to bring us through them.

You will handle these times better (never easily) if you truly make up your mind and settle in your heart, "Not as I will, but as Thou wilt." Then carry your cross as He did—without complaint.

If our people's faith is based on the assumption that a true Christian will never suffer, then when their fiery trial comes, as I Peter 4:12-13 says it will, they may not be able to stand. But if we will teach them to trust God throughout the ordeal and be thankful that He has a good reason (although not always understood by us), then we will have rock-sure saints with beautiful, uncomplaining spirits who can say as the Apostle Paul did in II Corinthians 12:9-10, "Most gladly therefore will I rather glory in my infirmities, that the power of Christ may rest upon me. Therefore I take pleasure in infirmities, in reproaches, in necessities, in persecutions, in distresses for Christ's sake: for when I am weak, then am I strong." The pain and the tears are not pleasant but the purpose is. "Wherefore let them that suffer according to the will of God commit the keeping of their souls to him in well doing, as unto a faithful Creator" (I Peter 4:19).

I am very happy to be a minister's wife and a missionary and I hope my role never changes, but to be truthful, I am not always overjoyed with what takes place at every given moment. I, too, know what sleepless nights of worry are all about. I've had my share of troublemaking members, I've worked on church projects with quarrelsome women, and I've taught home Bible studies for weeks only to be given a feeble excuse as to why the person can't serve the Lord. I have had to ask people, including some of my own church members, for forgiveness because I've spoken things I should not have said. I have been worried, depressed, angry, and jealous. I have felt guilty, frustrated, and scared. I've had some long struggles in prayer to get anger and bitterness out of my heart. I've been unable to think clearly enough even to pray or read my Bible.

Neither then nor now am I proud of these things, but how can I help you if I am not honest with you, if I pretend that I have never experienced such emotions and am above such feelings, or if I state that you can live above them if you will just try as hard as you should? While it is certainly true that we can overcome these things with the help of the Lord, just to pray and "snap out of it" is easier said than done. A few times I was afraid that if anything "snapped" it would be my mind.

Those who say that they have never experienced negative emotions have reached some kind of super-spiritual pinnacle that I have never known to exist, or else they have never been through what many others have had to face, such as losing a child in death, being cruelly and purposefully hurt by someone and honestly not knowing why, having an unfaithful husband, not knowing where their children's next meal was coming from, or a million other things that can severely try a person's soul. God can and will give victory over these things or anything else, but that does not mean the child of God may not have some very dark days, nights, seasons, and valleys to walk through, with nothing to hold to but trust in the Lord until the victory comes. The emotions of anger, jealousy, frustration, worry, guilt, depression, fear, and so on can and do come to the very best of God's people, and they do not mean that the person is a failure, has no faith, has disappointed God, or has backslidden. They simply mean that the child of God is temporarily in a fiery trial and needs the Lord, as well as the understanding and support of God's people, more than ever. Unrepented sin is all that will separate a person from God, not problems.

Elijah once prayed to die, the preacher in Ecclesiastes said that at one point he hated life, and King David was often at his wit's end and watered his couch with his tears.

From time to time everyone needs a good cry and should not condemn herself or allow others to accuse her of having a pity party.

Sometimes pressures, situations, or even painful memories can temporarily become too much for you and crying your eyes out will do wonders. Not until Jesus returns will all tears be forever wiped away; therefore when it is time to cry, have a good cry. Then get up and face the challenge.

It is not always necessary to try to cheer up someone who is suffering. Sometimes deep sympathy and understanding are much more appropriate—for instance, if someone has lost a loved one or a wife has been abandoned with little children to care for. Be sensitive and realistic concerning the situation, and express your understanding and sorrow for the person's hurt and suffering.

Guilt

Guilt is an emotion that we must sometimes deal with, whether in ourselves or in one of our people. Fleeting moments of guilt for speaking unnecessarily sharp to a child or napping too long and not completing some task are minor and can be readily handled, but a deeper sense of guilt and shame for something God has already forgiven must be overcome, or it will rob us of the deep joy and peace that the Lord wants us to have.

Many women today come to the Lord from a very sordid past. Guilt for past sexual sin, for example, may continue to plague them. Perhaps a woman had an abortion or gave a child up for adoption and is now filled with remorse. Many women's homes and childhoods were filled with sin, and ungodliness and ungodly people were their only models. Some women were simply rebellious and were deep in sin when Jesus came to the rescue and cleansed them.

God is love. He is full of compassion, understanding, and forgiveness. His ability to forgive a person is never the problem. The problem is often that a person is unable to forgive herself. Minor transgressions are sometimes done in ignorance, but the larger offenses are committed with knowledge that they are wrong, and that is what produces the horrible guilt. Knowing not to do something and yet choosing to do it anyway is what tears the conscience to pieces.

And who can claim that she has never done anything that she knew to be wrong? "If we say that we have not sinned, we make him a liar, and his word is not in us" (I John 1:10). The Lord knows that each of us has sinned willfully, but He forgives freely and still loves us.

Don't condemn others for their past, and don't let Satan condemn you for yours. When you repented of your own particular sins, were baptized in the wonderful name of Jesus and were filled with the precious Holy Ghost, God washed the guilt from your soul and from your record. He will never remind you of it or torment you with the failures and transgressions of the past. They are still in your memory, however, and Satan loves to torment you with them if you allow him to do so.

Some people have an absolutely shocking past and readily admit how dreadful they were, but knowing that God has forgiven them, they begin afresh and go their way rejoicing. They realize that they are now clean and free from their sin and guilt. This is by far the best attitude, although no one likes to see people practically bragging about how bad they were. This "I-am-forgiven" attitude is the one God wants the worst former sinner to have. He wants us to forgive ourselves as freely as He has forgiven us. What purpose could possibly be served by our continually being browbeaten by the past? We should lift up our heads, for when Jesus forgives, He forgives one hundred percent.

Mary Magdalene was once possessed by seven demons, which meant that she was probably never mistaken for Snow White; yet she had the honor of being the first person on earth to see Jesus after His resurrection. He met her in the garden, called her by name, and revealed Himself as the risen Christ. She then left to bring the message of the resurrection to the apostles. Jesus said of the woman who washed His feet with her tears and dried them with her hair, "Her sins, which are many, are forgiven; for she loved much" (Luke 7:47). He is not interested in sins that He has already cleansed and forgiven, nor does He care to see them constantly replayed in our mind. What He wants to know is, Do we love Him now?

It is a trick of the enemy to make you so conscious of your own shortcomings that your faith will be hindered. Guilt will make you think, God *can* do what I ask and He *would* do it for anyone else, but how could He possibly be willing to do it for me when He knows how unworthy I am? But God only wants your love, not a constant rehashing of your past. Refuse to indulge in any further self-chastisement and believe that when God said He forgave you that He was speaking the truth. Remember, it is impossible for Him to lie.

Many bad or unclean thoughts (and everyone has them) are from Satan. Having such a thought does not mean that you are horrible. Just reject it and get your mind on better things as quickly as possible. Never entertain bad thoughts, or they will return frequently.

Anger, Bitterness, and Jealousy

At times you may become angry and have a very good reason to do so, but keep it temporary—and sin not. (See Ephesians 5:26, 31.) Anger, if allowed to remain, turns to bitterness. Bitterness has to be rooted out, or it will lodge in a deep, secret place where you can almost forget it, and it will eventually destroy you. A person may dress up bitterness and grudges in clever disguises, declare that they are actually righteous indignation, and try to justify their existence in his heart, but God recognizes them no matter how cleverly that person has disguised them, and He rejects them.

Satan also recognizes bitterness and grudges. He will feed them and help them grow out of proportion until their roots destroy every other good seed. Not for the sake of your enemy, but for the sake of your own eternal soul, learn how to forgive freely, completely, and quickly.

If you do not, you will tie God's hands from forgiving you, for He has promised to forgive you in the same way that you forgive someone who has wronged you (Matthew 6:14-15). Wouldn't it be awful if God said that He forgave you and then told everyone how rotten you were? Is that forgiveness? If you still become upset, angry, or full of negative thoughts every time you think of a person or an incident, then you have not forgiven. Keep praying! It is only when the situation can pass through your mind without provoking you to anger that you have actually forgiven. It is possible, however, to forgive someone freely without placing yourself in a position to be hurt again if you know that they are likely to do so. If your neighbor kicks you, you can forgive him, but you don't need to go back for a daily kicking.

Godly jealousy such as Paul had for his people is fine, but an ugly, envious, suspicious spirit is not. It must be dispelled.

One of the best ways to overcome a negative or evil emotion is to admit to Jesus exactly how you feel. He knows anyway, so don't be too afraid or too proud to discuss it with Him. Be more afraid of trying to hide it from Him. Tell Him that your husband, neighbor, brother, or sister is driving you to despair, that you can't get over what so-and-so did to you, or whatever the problem is. Tell the Lord all about it and exactly how it is affecting you. Then (this is the hard part) tell Him with all sincerity that you will do *anything* He tells you to do in order to overcome this thing, that you will submit to His will, and that you will be faithful to His Word in working out the solution of your dilemma. Satan will offer you all kinds of solutions and even help you justify yourself, but only what is done according to the Word of God will actually solve the problem.

Submitting your will to God's will when it is painful to do so is your Gethsemane, and it is not easy. But neither was it easy for Jesus when He submitted His human will at Gethsemane and Calvary for you. Above all, don't forget to praise God in the midst of your problem, for in spite of the pain, you will become a better person if you will wholly accept His will and His solution.

One time, one of our church members said something derogatory about my husband in front of me and some other people. I didn't say anything, but it hurt me and made me very angry. I couldn't get over it for days. I didn't want to tell my husband and hurt him too, but finally I couldn't conquer it alone, so I told him all about it. His instant reaction was, "Go to her and apologize for the bad thoughts you have been having against her for this." My instant reaction was to think, "Why me? I didn't say anything wrong." But before I could say it, the Lord said to me, "You offended me, yet I came to you."

In that moment my anger vanished, and I felt very humbled. It was much easier to face her after I had faced the Lord. When I apologized for my anger against her, she burst into tears and asked me to forgive her, for she didn't mean what she said and didn't know what made her say it. The air was cleared completely, and I loved her even more than I had before. It truly pays to leave your gift at the altar and first be reconciled to your brother or sister (Matthew 5:24).

Negative emotions will come. This does not mean that we have to develop a liking for them, pet them, and invite them to stay and be our guide. They can lead to sin and more heartbreak if not overcome. Certain situations or circumstances may come that would be depressing for anyone, but we can't stay depressed forever. We must take certain painful steps as soon as we are able with the help of the Lord and do whatever is necessary to overcome the cause of the depression. Recognizing and naming the cause will help to define it and prevent it from growing and becoming all consuming. Sometimes the Lord gives miraculous victory in a moment's time over the deepest depression. At other times He brings the person out one struggling step at a time. It is His choice as to how He will help. He has His reasons, and He is sovereign. But He will bring us through every situation if we will have faith.

Moodiness

One evidence of uncontrolled emotions is extreme moodiness. Some people change their moods as often as they do their clothing, and woe to those around them if they happen to be in a bad mood. Some will snap and bite like an ill-tempered dog at anything that moves and breathes. Others will simply refuse to speak to anyone for a few hours or even a few weeks.

This behavior is hardly doing unto others as you would have them do to you, for no one wants to be snapped at and no one wants to be around someone who won't speak to them. I once had a neighbor who acted this way, and being friends with her was very difficult. One day she would be very friendly. The next day when I spoke to her she could appear to look right through me. She would not even acknowledge my existence.

If you behave in this manner and it is beyond your control, get counselling. But if you behave in this manner simply because you are so immature that you refuse to be considerate of others' feelings, then grow up. Ask the Lord for help before you ruin your own family relationship, your ministry to people, and possibly your husband's ministry. Some people use this silent treatment as a way to get even with those who have displeased them, but vengeance belongs to the Lord. You will answer to Him for the way you treat those around you.

Victory Despite Problems

With time, experience, and especially the help of the

Lord, you will learn to recognize these various negative emotions and their effects sooner and be able to control them more quickly. You will also learn to recognize them in others and to have more compassion for them instead of disgust, indignation, or disdain.

It is much easier for me to forgive others when I need it so often myself. I can love the unlovable more sincerely when I realize how unlovable I can be. I can have more patience with the stumblers since I have fallen so many times myself. God has again and again proved His long-suffering and patience with me. He has been willing to cleanse me repeatedly. He has given me His infinite, glorious grace, stood by me, and brought me through many situations when I so clearly demonstrated my unworthiness of His great love. He has asked me to forgive others seventy times seven, and I am so thankful that He will do no less for me. Since I have been, and still am, the recipient of so much patience and love, I want to give the same to others as freely as I have received from Him.

As a minister's wife, you are in a unique position to give in many ways, but the gift must come from your heart for it to be a true blessing to others. There is no substitute for sincerity. You can learn "charm" from books and be charming enough to entice a cobra out of his basket without a toot of the flute, but if you don't have warmth, sincerity, and genuine love for the Lord and His people, they will eventually detect it. They will not have confidence in you, they will lose respect for you, and your problems with them will multiply.

Even when you are not exactly feeling your best, you can still be courteous and give smiles, compliments (only sincere ones), comfort, encouragement, patience, understanding, talents, help with the workload, and especially love. Learn to handle your emotions so that you will be better equipped to help your members cope with theirs. Give to them as unto the Lord, with a willing heart, and you will reap accordingly. Then no matter what you or your members face, you will be ready, because Jesus is by your side and you can overcome anything with His help. When it is time to weep, weep unashamedly, and when it is time to laugh—have a ball!

In II Corinthians 4:8-9, Paul demonstrated how we can have victory in the midst of problems. We are

Troubled	but	Not distressed
Perplexed	but	Not in despair
Persecuted	but	Not forsaken
<u>Cast down</u>	<u>but</u>	<u>Not destroyed</u>

Total:
| Problems | but | Victory |

Specific Questions

Now let us continue with questions and answers about specific situations.

Depression

Is it normal for a MW (minister's wife) to have times of depression?

Yes, at times, for she is human, she is a woman and, besides, some situations are downright depressing. Depression is normal as long as it is caused by a particular trying circumstance and is not prolonged beyond reason.

If depression is prolonged or shows signs of deepening, get counselling from a qualified, Spirit-filled person. Don't ever be ashamed to admit depression and seek help, for often God uses others to bring us through our difficulties, and He will give you the victory again. Often those closest to you will find it difficult to have patience because your pain hurts them too, so try to find someone who is just a little bit removed from the situation and can be more objective.

While it is normal to be hurt by painful situations, be honest and check yourself for self-pity that may be getting out of bounds. Zero in on the cause and admit it. Then take whatever steps are possible to alter the situation. Some things cannot be changed (death of a loved one, your past, etc.), but just as soon as you are able, get busy. Get involved in life to keep from dwelling on the depressing situation and letting it get you too far down.

If the cause of the depression is unknown, check your physical health. Older women should have their estrogen checked. Even in North America people have been hospitalized for depression caused by poor diets—too much sugar, white flour, and overprocessed foods. When the body is deprived of the required nutrients that God designed it to have, mental health as well as physical health will eventually be affected. (For further study, see *God's Key to Health and Happiness* by Elmer A. Josephson.) Exercise that improves blood circulation is also beneficial for people who are depressed, for it is hard to be depressed when you are feeling great physically.

If your depression is not physically caused, is prolonged, or is deepening, then get counselling and be cooperative. Nothing is more frustrating than a person who balks and refuses to be helped.

Feelings of Inadequacy

Is it normal for some MWs to feel inadequate to be leaders?

Moses balked so much when God called him that the Lord finally sent Aaron to do his speaking. When the Lord told Jeremiah that He ordained him to be a prophet, Jeremiah responded, "Ah, Lord GOD! behold, I cannot speak: for I am a child" (Jeremiah 1:6). If men of their caliber felt inadequate to do what God asked of them, then surely it is normal for us to feel likewise.

In fact, the majority of us do feel inadequate at various times and in varying degrees, but it is possible to overcome those feelings of inferiority by prayer and by simply doing the best job we can until we gain confidence. There are also many books available at Christian bookstores on self-improvement, and they can help build confidence. But the greatest source of help should always be the Lord Himself and His Word. Any advice contrary to His Word should be rejected.

God never asks anyone to do something and then refuses to equip that person for the job. Trust His ability to choose the right person for the job, even when that person is you. Maybe He chose you because He knows that He will get the glory for what He will accomplish through you—if you give Him the chance.

An excellent book for people with low self-esteem is *What Wives Wish Their Husbands Knew About Women* by Dr. James Dobson.

Nervous Breakdowns

Can MWs have nervous breakdowns? What can we do to help each other?

Yes, unfortunately, MWs have nervous breakdowns. To guard against this, you must learn your own strengths and weaknesses and be honest with yourself about how much pressure you can handle. Do not allow yourself to take on too much responsibility, and do not allow others to make you feel guilty because you are not doing all that they think you should do. Only do as much as you can handle and still maintain your health and sanity.

Some people have a lot of drive, ambition, energy, and talent, and they can work circles around the rest of us. If you try to be like them and accomplish all they do, or compare yourself with them, you are going to be one frustrated little lady. (But if you happen to be one of those superproducers, have patience with the rest of us.) I have worked myself into a dither and nearly senseless simply because I felt guilty to admit that I couldn't handle something. Now I take much better care of myself.

Sometimes people or circumstances will get you down. If you cannot change something and it is not possible to avoid it (or them), you must pray diligently, fast if need be, and grit your teeth until it changes or you can cope with whatever, or whoever, it is. But at all times be honest with yourself about your own feelings. Don't pretend to yourself that all is well when something is too much to handle, and don't blame or criticize yourself for not being stronger or more capable. Admit it first to yourself and then to your husband, and then do what is necessary about the situation as fast as you are able.

Face to Face with Feelings

On the other hand, you must never deliberately and falsely claim to have a delicate nervous system just as an excuse to avoid doing God's work. God will know better, and if you deceive yourself you have only fooled a foolish woman.

I believe that you will want to do and endure all that you honestly can, but never be pushed into attempting more than you can handle. We all have our limits. God won't put more on us than we can bear, but sometimes we don't stop when He wants us to, and we drive ourselves too far.

Go out of your way to make friends of those MWs nearest you. This may not be easy. Lack of time is a hindrance. Also, many MWs have been hurt or have had to "go it alone" for so long that they are now withdrawn. As I have talked with MWs everywhere their saddest complaint is "I have no one to talk with" or "I have no real friend." We must all work together to overcome this lack, and the only way to do so is to take off our masks and begin to minister to one another.

Do you know or care if the MW near you has a friend? Please be one to her. Be willing to overcome the hindrances, the obstacles, and the facade she may put up. Sometimes the brightest smile hides the loneliest heart. You will never know unless you take the time and make the effort to be a friend.

Be sensitive, pay attention to the MWs around you, and give your help when they need it. Don't assume someone else is helping. You offer. Visit them to encourage them, or maybe just give them a telephone call to let them know that you are praying for them.

Keep confidences. Never betray a trust. Be someone

that others feel they can turn to and trust in their hour of need. To be this type of person you must never engage in any type of petty gossip.

Be a friend. I once received a small card from another local pastor's wife who wrote that she loved and appreciated me and was praying for me. What a lift that gave me, and it also caused me to love, appreciate, and pray more for her.

Stay out of problems that may arise between your husband and another minister. Why should wives quit speaking to each other because the men may have a problem? Let them work it out. Problems are only prolonged when women get involved unnecessarily.

Pastors' wives and evangelists' wives could and should be a real blessing to each other. A pastor's wife can help evangelists' wives by being well-prepared for their visits and making them feel welcome and appreciated. (Don't take it out on them if your husband invited them against your wishes.) Consider the difficulties of evangelizing, and provide enough food, a private place for the couple to sleep, and a decent bed for the children.

Bear in mind their children's emotional needs and the necessity of keeping as regular hours as possible. Try not to interfere too often in their school hours. Don't insist on their children attending every service if other arrangements can be made. Remember that they are in revival all year and need more nights off than adults. Be the kind of person the evangelist's wife can talk with and confide in if she has personal problems, and never repeat what she tells you. Try to be sensitive to her emotional and spiritual needs as well as her physical necessities.

An evangelist's wife can help the pastor's wife by not

taking advantage of her hospitality. Do what you can to lighten her load while you are there by helping with the work and sharing the responsibilities of the revival. Be willing to teach a class if requested to do so. Be sensitive to her needs, and never repeat what she tells you in private. Do your best to encourage her.

Be honest and ethical, and do not weigh her down by telling her how bad other churches and people are in your opinion. Speak only the good things of God, and you will uplift her spirits immeasurably. Make your children behave well, and do not allow them to be rude or destructive in her home. If they break something, you should pay for it, and if you use the telephone for long distance calls, be sure to pay for the charges before you leave.

Resentment

Is it normal to feel resentment at times for all of the demands put on a MW?

Resentment does happen, but you yourself choose to be resentful or not. Don't allow yourself to be put under demands that will cause you to become angry. Your husband cannot read your mind. Talk to him about the demands and your difficulty in handling them *before* you get angry about them, and if at all possible, he should lighten your load. Many wives continue to accept more and more duties and responsibilities and never say a word until they reach their limit. Then they either blow up or have a nervous breakdown. Speak up as soon as you begin to feel that things are getting too much for you—when you can still be nice about it.

Loneliness

Isn't it often lonely to be a MW if you can't spend too much time with an individual church member, your husband is gone a lot, and your relatives are far away?

Yes, many times you will feel lonely, and for some MWs this is the hardest part of their special calling. As your church grows and activities increase, you will learn to adjust, and it will bother you less and less.

The old saying is true: "An idle mind is the devil's workshop." Keep busy. Get involved. The Bible suggests ways to avoid idleness: visit widows and orphans, help the needy, serve others. If too much time is a problem, as it may be if your church is small or you have no children at home, look for ways to help others. Doing volunteer work for worthy causes, helping in hospitals, and so on are good ways to make contacts for your church, to get home Bible studies started, and to make a good impression on your community.

Read books that inspire and challenge you, including books on self-improvement. Take courses on baking, ceramics, or Egyptian mummies if that is what you like. Develop a hobby that you enjoy, but never just sit. If you don't fill your time, Satan will find something for you to do.

Chapter Two

Relationship With Your Husband

There is an ugly spirit in the world today that is pitting women against men and destroying thousands of homes, families and lives. Only those who look to Jesus for the answers have protection from this satanic plague. Many Spirit-filled people have taken their eyes off the Lord, trying to take matters in their own hands and work out problems in their own way, and today they are suffering the tragic consequences. Formerly strong marriages, among them many marriages of ministers and their wives, are today in shambles because the partners—one or both—stopped guiding their home by God's principles and started demanding their rights and wanting to do their own thing. Some became full of anger, let resentments build up until they would listen to no one, and willfully disregarded God's Word to the destruction of their own family.

God's plan always has been and always will be for the husband to be the head of the family. He is to love his wife as Christ loved the church and be willing to die for her if need be (Ephesians 5:25). He is to protect her and provide for her and the children the necessities of life, whether they be material, emotional, or spiritual. I Timothy 5:8 says, "But if any provide not for his own, and specially for those of his own house, he hath denied the faith, and is worse than an infidel." We should note, however, that he is to provide the necessities—not cater to his wife's every whim and desire. The Bible also warns the husband that if he is not good to his wife and does not treat her honorably then his prayers will be hindered (I Peter 3:7). God does not approve of a man who mistreats his wife.

The husband must fulfill his responsibilities, treating his family with love, courtesy, and kindness, if the marriage is to be all that God intends for it to be. The wife cannot make the marriage a success by herself; the husband must cooperate in the effort. In God's eyes the husband and wife become "one flesh" (Genesis 2:24). They are to blend together and harmonize, to be of equal value and worth, and to complement and complete one another. The only difference between them is the roles they fulfill.

The Husband's Role

Ephesians 5:25, 28 says, "Husbands, love your wives, even as Christ also loved the church, and gave himself for it. . . . So ought men to love their wives as their own bodies. He that loveth his wife loveth himself."

How does Christ love the church, and how does He manifest His love for us? When our actions or words displease Him, He never yells at us, but He gently corrects us in love. When we are late and procrastinate in doing what He has asked of us, He treats us with much patience and longsuffering. When we make mistakes He gently and patiently teaches us and never makes fun of our errors or tells others how stupid we are. When we fail and sin against Him and ask for forgiveness, He forgives us quickly and sincerely. He never throws a fit, brings up the past, or makes ugly accusations. He does not swell up, pout and refuse to speak or listen to us, nor does He storm off in anger and leave us alone. When we need correction He corrects us with the utmost love and concern for us, and He does it in private. He never causes us embarrassment or criticizes us in front of others.

The Lord does let the whole world know that we are the apple of His eye and that in His eyes we are beautiful and precious. He keeps His promises and sticks closer than a brother. He is faithful to us and stands behind us when the going is rough. He understands when we cry and never belittles our tears or discouragements. He consoles and encourages us with tender mercy when we fail or feel depressed.

Jesus also helps us to carry our burdens and perform our tasks. He would never ask too much of us or sit by idly while we try to perform our duties. He will never leave us nor forsake us but is always loyal and steadfast, especially when we are in a storm, and He would never ridicule our fears or make a joke of them. In actions as well as in words He is always kind and gentle with us. His dedication to providing our necessities ultimately cost Him His life.

This, then, is how Jesus loves the church and how a husband is commanded to love his wife. It takes a real man to be kind and gentle as well as strong, and Jesus is the perfect example. David said about the Lord, "Thy gentleness hath made me great" (Psalm 18:35). If a man wants his wife to be great, he needs to be gentle and considerate in the way he treats her.

He should also be careful never to allow anyone, especially their children, to treat or talk to her disrespectfully or hurt her feelings. A husband should shield and defend his wife. A man may buy his wife the moon, but if his actions and words are sharp, bossy, critical, ridiculing, or negligent concerning her feelings, he cannot expect her to be happy. The Lord did not intend for this subject to become a joke, and every man will some day give an account to Him as to how he obeyed the commandment to love his wife as Jesus loves the church.

Most women who are treated correctly have no trouble submitting to their husbands' leadership and fulfilling their half of the responsibility for a happy home. They happily look forward to their husband's coming home and try to make home a pleasant place for him.

But, wives, if your husband has not yet learned how to treat you, be patient with him and keep reading to see if there are a few improvements that you could make so that he will *want* to treat you better.

To be the head of a family, to be responsible for the family's spiritual, financial, and emotional well-being, and to protect the family is no easy matter. Every husband will give an account to God concerning how he fulfilled his task. It would have been most unfair if God had given him these responsibilities but no authority to fulfill them. Can you imagine someone who owns a large business telling his manager, "I will hold you personally responsible for the operation of my business, and you must answer to me if it does not succeed; however, the employees don't have to do what you tell them to do unless they jolly well want to do it." It would never work. A person with responsibility must have corresponding authority. He must be in control of the situation or chaos will result.

The responsibility to provide for the family is quite a load—not a treat—that the Lord has placed on a husband's shoulders, as many women who are trying to raise their children without a husband are discovering. Just earning the money is quite a weight to carry in itself. Then there is the burden of important decisions as well as minor daily decisions. Should the family stay here or move to another city? What should be done about Johnny's reading? Does Susie really need braces? Should the family get a piano for all the kids to have lessons? Can the family afford the lessons? Should a needy relative be allowed to move in? Of course, the wife should voice her opinion on these matters and share in the decision-making process. The husband should respectfully consider her views, but the ultimate decision and the consequences of the decision are upon his shoulders. The wife is relieved of the final decision so that she may more efficiently discharge her own responsibilities.

These obligations are daily weights that men must bear in addition to the common worries such as, What if I lose my job? Who will support my family? Rarely is a young minister financially secure for life. It is a terrible trial for a man whose wife must earn the living, and most godly men shudder at the thought of losing a job and having to be supported by a woman. Then there is the maintenance and repair of cars, houses, washing machines, and tricycles, and the mowing of the lawn. Some can afford to hire others to do these things, but the majority of young men wind up doing them after their regular job whether they know how to or not. If they are lucky, a friend who may know a little more may come over and help. Some men do all these things and more with their wife screeching, "Why don't you help me with these kids?"

If you are just terrific and are already doing your share and most of his, and he still won't cooperate, get personal counselling.

Understanding Your Husband

Just being married is not enough to insure a good life. Both husband and wife must work at the marriage daily. If the husband will fulfill all that God requires of him, and if the wife will guide the daily affairs of the home and children and take care of her husband, life can be worth living. When either one shirks his or her responsibility or tries to butt in on the other's territory, problems arise. There will always be frustrations, disagreements, and irritations in even the most loving of families, but these can be overcome as long as each person stays in his or her own God-given role. Sometimes, due to extraordinary circumstances, one partner must carry the other's load, but this should only be temporary if at all possible.

If the wife takes over the husband's responsibility unnecessarily, she actually belittles his ability. If he refuses certain of his tasks, it may be because his wife has made him feel inadequate, in which case the best favor the wife could do for him is to encourage him and convince him that he is capable. While each partner should always be willing to help the other in times of need, neither should demand it from the other on a continuing basis. A wife

Relationship with Your Husband

should not be forced to earn the living unless absolutely necessary, nor should she have to make the difficult decisions.

On the other hand, a husband should not have to come in from a day's work and spank the children for something the wife should have already handled. "Just wait till your daddy comes home and you are going to catch it" is no way to raise his image in their eyes. The mother should handle a discipline problem when it happens unless it is something of a very serious nature or unless the father is present, in which case either could correct the child, depending on the situation.

Both parents should be involved in the correction of children as well as in the decisions concerning them. Neither should habitually make the other appear to be the "bad guy." They should back up each other in decisions and not make remarks such as "I would let you, but you heard your father (or mother)." Moreover, just as a husband should never allow the children to speak to or treat their mother disrespectfully or in a way that would hurt her feelings, neither should the mother allow children to speak disrespectfully of their father when he is not present.

No man is perfect any more than any woman is, but no wife should have to live with abuse either to herself or her children, not even constant verbal abuse. If this occurs in your case, then please get personal counselling from a Spirit-filled person and do something about your situation. A woman does have her place, but it is by her husband's side, not under his feet. However, this book does not deal with those who preach hypocritically and deliberately mistreat their wives, but rather with those who honestly and sincerely try to do the will of God as best they can and try to keep their family well and happy. In other words, we will only discuss normal, precious, Spirit-filled husbands who drive their wives up the wall at times with irritating ways and habits.

Men and women are different in many ways, and until you learn to accept and adjust to your spouse and his particular way of doing things, his manner of speaking, his moods and what causes them, and how he reacts to various things, you are going to have some touchy times. Remember that he also must learn to adjust to what he may consider your weird way of doing things and your reactions to situations. One thing you should both strive for is not to be "down" at the same time. If he is in a low state of mind, be kind and understanding, but don't be excessively cheerful and chattery, or he may wish that he could clobber you. If a person is depressed, excessively cheerful people get on his nerves, and if he is in a happy mood, someone who is down is irritating. So try to balance his moods but not in the extreme. Both of you should avoid extreme moodiness.

We ladies are usually either thrilled or hurt by things most men would not even notice. I have yet to meet the husband who lies awake at night wondering if he is pleasing his wife or a man who reads books and magazines galore on the subject of marriage. Some wives are long gone before the husband realizes that there is a problem. Men just don't think as we do, and if you ever get your husband to think and act as you do (as a woman) you will have a real mess on your hands. We feel, react, and demonstrate things differently. Now tell the truth, would your husband burst into tears of joy if you brought him

Relationship with Your Husband

a dozen roses just because you love him? Even if you surprised him with a fishing rod, chances are he would ask another preacher to go fishing with him instead of you.

Do your best to accept him "as is," including his flaws. Whatever you do, wait for an appropriate time to discuss those things that upset you too much to be ignored. Not all things should be overlooked; if you attempt to overlook all of his faults, you will become either a doormat or a seething volcano of angry resentment. But accept what you can, and don't launch an attack about what you can't adjust to. Wait until you are calm enough to discuss the problem without yelling and accusing.

Most husbands generally accept wives as they are. They may complain about some things, but rarely does a man try to remake his wife completely. And when one does try, he usually fails.

Unfortunately, there are some nagging husbands who continually complain about everything their wife does. Nothing she does is fast enough, soon enough, or done correctly. Then this same foolish, nagging, complaining husband is surprised when she begins turning her back on him at night. Although a mature woman knows better than to use sex as a reward or to withhold it as punishment, it is understandable that a woman whose husband cannot be pleased all day will not be eager to please him at night. A successful love life is created by around-the-clock mutual kindness and consideration, and only in this way can it be enjoyed by both as God intended.

But assuming that your husband is not a nag, you will want to listen for cues concerning changes you could make that would please him. Wear your hair the way he likes, maybe lose weight, wear your hair down at night if he asks, or use the perfume he likes. Little things can make a big difference. Be as careful about keeping him as you were about catching him. P.S. Get rid of that nightgown that he just despises, and use your pretty ones.

Don't try to keep score on who did what for or to whom. Your relationship with your husband won't be fifty-fifty everyday. Sometimes the ratio will be ninety-ten in your favor; sometimes ninety-ten in his favor. Sometimes it will be sixty-forty and so on. On occasion one may even give the whole one hundred percent, but over a lifetime things will generally balance out.

Most normal, God-fearing husbands are exasperating in a million ways but awfully sweet in two million others and are really worth keeping around, so thank God for yours. See if you can't spoil him a little bit with good housekeeping, cooking, and loving, and wrap his heart around yours in the process. Always remember that love cannot be demanded or obtained by pitiful pleadings; it must be earned.

Any husband carries a tremendous load of responsibilities, but a minister has a heavier load than most. The MW does also, but for a moment let's continue to concentrate on him. If you are a new MW, your husband is probably young and still working on a secular job in addition to being a minister. If he is known to be a preacher, he will be watched in every situation. A truck driver can become angry and cause a nasty scene in public without condemning all other truck drivers. Not so a minister. He not only has his own reputation but also the office of the ministry itself to protect. Let him make a slip and people sagely nod their heads, saying, "See what I mean; all preachers are a bunch of hypocrites." Therefore, your husband must always strive to keep a good spirit everywhere he goes, even in the most trying circumstances.

The worst sinners in town who have never read the Bible "know" how your husband should conduct himself, and woe unto him if he fails to measure up to their expectations. All day long, wherever he goes he has to walk on eggs. His co-workers demand perfection or else they will lose respect for him. And yet the same people will often subject him to little tests to see if he is genuine or just another hypocrite.

He is the constant target of Satan, who would love to stop him in order to keep him from helping others to find salvation. The devil will attack him, trying to destroy his self-confidence, bruise his ego, discourage him and make him feel like a failure. Satan will try to make him angry enough to use poor judgment and will tempt him with many things, among them money and other women. If the devil can destroy your husband, that leaves you and your children more vulnerable to his attacks.

Many days, by the time a man reaches his front door he has, in addition to his physical labor, encountered countless battles, although they may have lasted only a few moments each. The majority were fought in his own mind and spirit. Upon wearily arriving at his front door, what can he look forward to on the other side? An empty house because the wife wants to earn money for a few extra luxuries or to "fulfill" herself? No dinner? A messy house? Or maybe an angry wife because he again forgot to mail a letter or stop by the cleaners on the way home? Hungry, whining kids? A recital of all that has gone wrong in the house all day, for which he is to blame? If this is what he finds, his wife is helping Satan to drive him away, possibly right out of the house or even the church.

Or when he opens the door can he find a place of refuge to restore his failing energy and ego? Will he find a pleasant wife who is wise enough to refresh him and strengthen him before adding to his load, if this be necessary? Would it really be too much to expect a good meal, some affection from his wife and children, maybe even some encouraging words and some laughter?

Be the kind of wife who will make your husband glad that he fought well today and resisted all the enemy threw at him. If you are not, he could be overwhelmed and give up the fight without ever even realizing why he decided to quit.

The kind of reception your husband gets is in your hands, and your relationship with him sets the mood for the whole family. Just knowing that God wants you to do these things and knowing how much they help your man should be reward enough. He will be thankful and enjoy his homecomings even if he doesn't know how to express his feeling in words.

It is true that some men can be terribly thoughtless. One lady I know is always clean, but one day she worked especially hard on her house. She shined, waxed, polished, cleaned windows, and cooked a beautiful dinner for her husband, who was not a Christian. When he came home, her eyes were shining with accomplishment as she smilingly asked, "Well, how does the house look?" He looked the shining house over very carefully then noticed the one thing that she had overlooked. Pointing high on the wall to an air vent over the kitchen stove, he said, "Why didn't you clean that vent?" How she kept from killing him, I will never know, but I do know that he never made *that*

Relationship with Your Husband

mistake again.

The more freely you express your gratitude for all your husband does for you, the more likely that he will eventually learn to express his appreciation for you. But there is no guarantee. Some never do, while others are wonderfully vocal about their appreciation. You may have to ask your husband every time if he is pleased with something, or learn to judge by other means. Sometimes all a man can muster up is a pat on the shoulder to express his thanks. Learn your man, and don't expect him to be like someone else.

I once told my husband how nice he looked just as we were leaving the house. He merely answered, "Thank you." I had to tell him, "That was your cue to tell me how nice I look." This he dutifully did, and with some laughter we were on our way. Fortunately, though, he rarely has to be cued. I also never take chances on being hurt by having him forget my birthday or our anniversary, so I begin a few weeks early by telling him how many shopping days he has left. He has many things on his mind and could possibly forget, and then I could be justified in feeling like a martyr and pouting or crying, but I find the good-humored approach to be much better.

Self-pity should not be a factor in the MW's behavior. The young MW needs to put away childish behavior and do her best to mature. If she acts like a child, she will be treated like a child, but if she can grow up she will not only be his wife but also his very best friend, with whom he will enjoy spending his time.

However, the wife should not be selfish with her husband. He needs men friends and opportunities to be alone with them occasionally without his wife becoming jealous or feeling mistreated. He needs men with whom he can go places and do things that do not interest his wife.

Don't smother your husband. Some men have to take their friends out to the garage or somewhere just to get away from their wife, so don't be pushy and refuse to let him spend some time alone with someone else. You enjoy talking with ladies without him, so give him the same opportunity with his friends.

If your marriage is already having problems, it may take quite a while to get the relationship turned around, but if you want a contented home instead of a broken one, it is at least worth a try. Get personal counselling if need be. If you really do love the Lord and your husband, and I am sure you do, then be willing to go even more than the second mile to take care of him. If he is normal, he will in turn love and appreciate you more and want to do more for your happiness.

The Other Man

Your husband will never be without flaws, but neither will any other man in whom Satan may try to interest you. The better you become acquainted with the other man, the more likely you are to learn about his annoying characteristics.

A woman once told me of being severely tempted to leave her husband for a man she had become acquainted with outside the church. Her husband's faults were magnified in her eyes to gigantic proportions and he seemed to be just short of a beast, while the other man appeared to be the ideal man in every way. Fortunately she confided in a couple of godly, reliable people who prayed with her, counselled her without condemning her,

Relationship with Your Husband

and kept her temptation confidential. After a long, hard struggle with their continued support, God touched her one night in a service and the temptation vanished. She could again see clearly to appreciate her fine husband's qualities, and the very sight of the cigarette-smoking other man was revolting to her.

She is not the only one to be tempted in such a manner, nor will she be the last. It is not always a sinner man with whom a MW may be tempted. It may be someone in the congregation or even another minister. If the enemy can accomplish the latter he can damage four ministries—those of both husbands and both wives.

Beware when the thought of seeing another man makes you go out of your way in order to do so, or when you begin to dress a little nicer and smile a little brighter for another man than you do for your own husband. Don't be ashamed to get counsel for anything Satan may try to trick or lure you into doing. Remember that he usually starts with very innocent, seemingly harmless methods.

It is no sin or indication of carnality to be tempted, for even Jesus was tempted in all points, but never toy with temptation. It only becomes sin when you surrender in your heart or in your deeds. You have already surrendered in your heart if the only thing keeping you from a sinful act is the opportunity to fulfil the desire. As long as you fight and pray to overcome that desire, you are still on the winning side.

Instead of looking around at someone who seems to be a better man than your husband, work hard to adjust to your husband's ways and habits and his manner of speaking. God did not authorize you to change him. Without a doubt your husband is also being driven up the wall occasionally by a few of your own habits and imperfections. (True, of course, that you are not as irritating as he can be—all of us wives understand *that*.) But if you can love him for his many good points, then learn to live with his flaws and pour some more honey on your marriage. There will be a lot less friction, and your family life will be happier, smoother and sweeter. In time you will realize that his flaws are not as horrible as you may have thought.

Chapter Three

Being a Good Wife

It is of utmost importance that a MW *learn* to be a good wife, for it does not happen automatically, nor does it happen overnight. She will enhance or cripple her husband's ministry by her attitudes and actions, with souls being brought to or turned away from the church in the process.

Your relationship with God is most important, and you will face Him all alone and answer for your attitude. Proverbs 16:2 says, "All the ways of a man are clean in his own eyes; but the LORD weigheth the spirits." Your attitude and spirit will be judged as well as your works. It is not possible to have a right relationship with God while having a bad attitude and exhibiting poor behavior toward your husband.

Strive to complement his ministry instead of struggling to compete or to be in the limelight. Proverbs 31 describes a virtuous woman with beautiful characteristics, and then says in verse 23 that it is her husband who is known in the gates. We find her taking care of the family, not down at the gates trying to take his place and run things. Likewise, a wise wife today will keep her husband propped up, oiled, wound and running smoothly so the people will think he is wonderful. She will listen to him and make helpful suggestions, which he knows he is free to accept or reject without making her angry, to help him become known for his wisdom. She will bear with him and help him through his times of discouragement, anger, and sadness in private so that he can be respected for his great disposition.

You may think that your patience, conduct, and helpfulness in private are unknown, and the details may actually be hidden, but people somehow know and appreciate a good woman, and they recognize when a man's ministry is helped or hindered by his wife. In time, the part that you play in building up or tearing down your man will become public knowledge. Some wives, especially today, balk at building up their husband and instead try to enhance their own image and belittle him, but they usually only succeed at losing people's respect. When such a woman loses her husband's love, it will be her own fault.

The woman who constantly supports her husband and whose conduct faithfully and consistently demonstrates her love and loyalty to him will become loved and respected by others. Proverbs 31:30-31 assures us, "Favour is deceitful, and beauty is vain: but a woman that feareth the LORD, she shall be praised. Give her of the fruit of her hands; and let her own works praise her in the gates." Her labors become known in the gates and praised even though she performs them in the home and for her family. Therefore, for the sake of your husband, family, marriage, church, Lord, personal happiness, and good name (Proverbs 22:1 says, "A good name is rather to be chosen than great riches"), it pays to be a loyal, hard-

Being a Good Wife

working wife. Even more importantly, you can save your own soul by being content in your role and not allowing hardness or bitterness to creep into your heart. In every way be the woman your man needs. Just as you should do everything, help your husband as though doing it unto the Lord. Woman was created to be a helpmate to her husband, so ask the Lord to anoint your ministry to him.

Practical Guidelines for Being a Good Wife

The following are a few practical guidelines for handling your daily responsibilities in the home, particularly with respect to your husband. I will only briefly mention each one, for you are probably already doing most of them. This is also an A to Z list of why it is better for a MW not to work outside the home unless it is necessary.

A. To begin with, feed your husband well. As we all know, a hungry man can be a cranky man. Most men actually enjoy bragging about their wife's cooking even if they seldom tell her.

Any human body operates better and breaks down less if its nutritional needs are met, so do a little studying and learn to cook with health in mind. Meals don't have to be fancy to be healthy and pleasant. But the best meal in the world is like sawdust if Mrs. Sourpuss sits on the other side of the table, so feed him well and be pleasant company.

B. Don't make your husband dread to come home, knowing that he will be greeted with anger about one thing or another and with a list of your day's woes and his failure to handle them. If he dreads it often enough or badly enough he eventually will find reasons simply not to come home.

C. Have dinner ready on time. Start early as possible. Hungry kids whine and are miserable. Feed them if he is late so he won't come home to cranky children. Some women go through misery every evening with crying kids and fussing husbands simply because they never have the food ready on time.

D. Know his schedule and his plans for the evening, and be ready. How many needless battles take place enroute to somewhere because the wife is always late! Try to get the children's clothes ready as early as possible so you won't be late because you couldn't find Susie's dress socks.

E. If you know that he is no help in getting the children dressed or into bed, then don't continually expect it and wait for it; just go ahead and do it yourself. Maybe his virtues lie elsewhere, and besides, this is really your job.

F. Keep his clothes ready and in good repair. He will be looked at and carefully scrutinized by many people, and he knows it. Don't make him wish that he could hide in a hole because of missing buttons, tears, dingy shirts, and so on. Even a poor man can feel at ease and confident if his clothes are neat and in good repair, although they may not be fancy. Why advertise your lack of funds through plain negligence?

G. It really pays to keep up your own appearance. Get dressed and comb your hair reasonably early, and try to wear your hair the way your husband likes it. Your husband will probably see many attractive women during the day, and even if you are no beauty, you don't want him to be sorry that he chose you. You also represent your church, and your members should be able to be proud of their pastor's wife. A sloppy woman will make them ashamed. It is not vanity to be as neat and attractive as you can. It does become vanity when you dress extravagantly, use ornaments, become excessively proud of yourself, or have a haughty attitude. (See Isaiah 3:16-17; I Timothy 2:9.) Eat right, exercise, and keep yourself as well groomed as the day's circumstances allow.

H. Don't run up a lot of bills that keep your husband worried or depressed and cause him to miss special functions. Don't keep your husband from attending conferences because you can't afford for both of you to go. It is very important that he be able to attend as many as possible to learn, to take part in the voting, and to be spiritually fed. Being short of money is no disgrace, but being the unnecessary cause of it certainly is.

The fewer charge cards you have, the better. By the time you pay interest on your balance, your bargains cease to be bargains.

Protecting your credit rating is very important. Everyone in the ministry should be very careful always to pay their debts. It is a shameful reproach to the house of God for a minister not to pay his bills. If you can't meet a payment, you or your husband should go to your creditor, explain the circumstance, and arrange to pay it as soon as you are able. Never leave town and refuse to pay the debts you left behind. Word about your dishonesty will spread far and wide.

I. Don't put things off until later if you can do them in the morning. You of all people never know when something unexpected is going to take place. In fact, you should expect the unexpected.

J. Love your husband enough and be sufficiently concerned for his feelings that you never complain to him about what you do not have, and never make comparisons to what someone else does have. God will bless you in His own time. Why make your husband feel bad and inferior because he cannot provide for you things that your family or friends have? Even subtle remarks and hints can hurt him deeply. I am sure he wants to do better, and eventually he probably will. Proverbs 28:16 promises those who do not always want more and more, "He that hateth covetousness shall prolong his days." How long would you like to live?

K. Control your temper. Being high tempered is a fruit of the flesh and *must* be overcome. Nothing is more miserable than being with someone when you never know what little thing is going to cause them to explode. Never embarrass or shame your husband by displaying a bad temper in front of others. Proverbs 12:4 tells us, "A virtuous woman is a crown to her husband: but she that maketh ashamed is as rottenness in his bones."

The Bible admonishes us to control anger. "He that is soon angry dealeth foolishly" (Proverbs 14:17). "He that hath no rule over his own spirit is like a city that is broken down, and without walls" (Proverbs 25:28). "The discretion of a man deferreth his anger; and it is his glory to pass over a transgression" (Proverbs 19:11). In other words, it is a glory to refuse to become angry when someone transgresses against you, and simply to ignore the wrong shows good judgment. How much better this is than flying off the handle over things.

Many other verses of Scripture teach that a high temper is something to overcome—not to brag about or to use as a weapon to get our own way. "He that is slow

Being a Good Wife

to wrath is of great understanding" (Proverbs 14:29). "He that is slow to anger appeaseth strife" (Proverbs 15:18).

As the wife of a minister and an example to the majority of your church members, you cannot indulge the flesh and allow your temper to rule you. You must rule it.

L. Resolve disputes and arguments promptly and in an adult fashion. I once met a man who was not a Christian who told me that he and his wife had been married for thirteen years and had never had even a small argument. I didn't believe it, and when I met his wife she proved I was right. I complimented her on a piece of furniture, and she furiously answered, "I despise it. I want another type of furniture but his mother likes this type so we have to get this type. He won't buy anything without her approval, and we go around and around about it all the time." Quite a different story, don't you think? I am still very doubtful when people say that they *never* have any disagreements. If it is true, how boring and how bored they must be. Nevertheless, when you are angry (as is bound to happen at least occasionally), don't attempt to discuss the dispute at the wrong time.

One darling MW told me that while she was talking with a group of church members before service her husband came up and, without saying a word to her, snapped his fingers and pointed at the piano to tell her to go to her place so the service could begin. She said it instantly made her furious for him just to snap his fingers at her, as if she were an animal that was beneath being spoken to. She had a huge wrestling match with her feelings to keep her anger from coming through the piano and ruining the service for everyone. Fortunately, she won the battle with her feelings and treated him normally until they were at home and in private, and then she let him know exactly how she felt. He had meant nothing disrespectful by his fingersnapping but was only trying to get her attention. He was amazed that she was angry and apologized for his thoughtlessness. She could have refused to speak to him, pounded the piano, or refused to play and stirred up all kinds of bad spirits, but by the time they got home he would have been so angry that he probably would have preferred to die rather than apologize for what he had done in innocence. By behaving as she did and waiting, she was able to see that she had no real cause to become so angry, and the matter was settled. "In your patience possess ye your souls" (Luke 21:19)—and your marriage.

If at all possible, try not to discuss your grievances when either of you is tired, hungry, pressed for time, in the presence of other people (including your children of any age), or expecting guests. At these times he is not likely to have much patience to try to see your point. Neither should you clam up and give him the cold shoulder. Such behavior is very childish. Be as pleasant as possible until there is time and opportunity to discuss the problem. If the problem is serious, go for a drive and park somewhere if need be so that you won't be interrupted (and take a hanky).

Some incidents are much more difficult to settle than others but try not to go to bed angry. Of course, it sometimes happens that a quarrel doesn't even begin until you are already in the bed, but at least try to settle it before you go to sleep. Isn't it miserable as you try not to let even your little toe touch him and both of you are lying on extreme opposite sides of the bed? Just as soon

Being a Good Wife

as you hear him snoring, you get even more angry because he can sleep so soundly while you are so upset. There you have it! Proof that he is an unfeeling clod who doesn't love you at all, or he couldn't sleep at a time like this. You toss and turn, or maybe you go to the couch and manage to drop off to sleep just before time to get up. The problem is still unresolved, and you feel even less like discussing it reasonably. He may even go off to work and leave you to stew in your own juices all day, during which time you will have a thousand imaginary arguments with him in which you really tell him off good.

The situation never works out as you have planned in your mind, however. The longer it is left unresolved, the harder it is to work out and the more miserable you both become. How much better it is to settle the problem quickly even if it means apologizing when you think he was more to blame than you. It is not the will of God to drag quarrels out interminably. No one should be angry very long, least of all those who are to teach others how to live for the Lord.

(P.S. The fact that he can sleep when you can't does not mean he does not love you; it is just another indication of the differences between men and women. Men usually just know that they have another hard day tomorrow and will settle the problem later.)

Even more important than not going to sleep angry is never going to church while you are angry. There are far more important issues at stake there than who is right or wrong between the two of you. At least call a truce if the problem is too serious to be solved quickly or completely. One young wife once told me that she arrived for service still angry at her husband, and as a result she wouldn't join in the congregational singing lest he see her and think she was no longer angry. Do you really think God is pleased with such actions? Please do your best never to make it necessary for your husband to go to the pulpit emotionally upset because of you. But don't give up on yourself if it sometimes happens in spite of your best intentions.

M. Don't be a constant chatterbox or interrupt your husband when he tells something. Above all, never correct him in front of others. A regional field supervisor for foreign missions told me that the foreign missions board would not appoint a man as a missionary if they knew he had a wife who corrected him in front of others. Even little insignificant matters should be left as stated by him. Who cares if your trip took two days or three, or if your new table was delivered on Tuesday or Wednesday? A wife who continually corrects her husband makes him look either untruthful or very foolish and makes herself look domineering. If you have this habit, it would be a good thing to break it.

N. Save cute little nicknames and baby talk for private, and call him by his last name in church.

O. Put your husband first before all others, including mother, father, and children. You will be with him more years than you will be with your children, and your contentment with him will make your children more emotionally stable and secure. You actually hurt your own children when you take their side against their father. Children need to have respect for their father, but how can they if the mother always points out his mistakes, reverses his orders, does things behind his back, or belittles him? If he really is such a terrible father, then get

Being a Good Wife

personal counselling, but don't constantly undermine him.

The Word of God teaches a woman to forsake all others and cleave only to her husband, so don't prevent yours from going to a city where he feels God has called him (even if you don't feel the call) because you don't want to leave your mom and dad. I fear some MWs will have to answer for souls who were lost because they refused to move and follow their husband, whether they lacked confidence in their husband, wouldn't leave their mom and dad, refused to give up a good job, or some other reason. Maybe they didn't like the city he felt called to or didn't like the schools. Whatever the reason, it should never take precedence over the call of God.

P. Never betray what your husband tells you in private, whether it be about himself, his family, or others. Especially do not disclose to others what he reveals to you about his innermost feelings, fears, and very personal experiences. If you plan on keeping him, plan on keeping his confidences. Only in this way can you assure him that he can trust you with anything. It is essential that he can trust you enough to tell you anything about anybody and know beyond a shadow of a doubt that you will never repeat what he has told you to anyone.

Q. Loving him as you do, you will not want to belittle him even with jokes. "Did I tell you what a dumb thing George did yesterday?" is a good way to tear your man down. If he wants it told, let him tell it.

R. Whether we like it or not, we absolutely must learn when to be silent. Many men, after they have preached a sermon that seemed to be an absolute dud (and this happens to the best of them), would prefer that the wife simply be quiet. Helpful suggestions for the next time are not needed now. He is far more concerned about, and therefore more sensitive to, your opinion than that of the entire congregation. You are also the only one he can go to and ask, "How did I do?" or "How was it?" If it truly was not one of his best, try to find something good to say, but don't criticize at that moment, no matter how much he insists that he knows it was a real bomb. More than likely the will of God was accomplished even if mankind wasn't thrilled.

God does not need great orators to get His message across. Can you imagine her reaction if Jonah had had a wife with him when he finally reached Nineveh? Mrs. Jonah: "Is that all you are going to preach to these people? 'Yet forty days, and Nineveh shall be overthrown.' I'm so embarrassed I could die. They don't even know what you are talking about. You can go sit on the hill under a plant if you want, but after that ridiculous sermon, I am going back to the hotel."

How about Peter's wife: "Peter, I do wish you would quit speaking so offensively to the Jewish leaders at the synagogue. Maybe if you would show a little more love and diplomacy you could win them over and quit getting thrown in jail."

If John the Baptist had a wife she probably would have been very dedicated to follow him into the wilderness and share his limited diet, but even such a woman would have shuddered when she heard him calling the religious leaders snakes and vipers and refusing to baptize them. No doubt she would have made reservations for him to attend the next seminar on "How to Have More Charisma and Show More Love."

Can you imagine what Nehemiah's wife would have

Being a Good Wife

thought upon learning that Brother Nehemiah had gotten so angry at some people that, in his own words, "I contended with them, and cursed them, and smote certain of them, and plucked off their hair," and "Therefore I chased him from me" (Nehemiah 13:25, 28)? If your husband does not always preach or behave exactly as you feel he should have, stand by him anyway; it may be that he has done or said precisely what God wanted him to do or say.

The preachers in the Bible never hesitated to call sin just what it was, so if your husband must perform a little surgery to cut some sin out of hard hearts, you just be there to pour on the oil and wine after the service to let the people know how very much they are loved. We still need strong preachers, and wives to back them in the fight.

It could be that your husband will never be an eloquent, dynamic preacher. Some ministers are, but not all. But some of the worst speakers make the very best pastors, while some camp-meeting preachers are not very effective as pastors. The majority of pastoral work is not done in the pulpit but rather in private visits, homes, hospitals, and prisons and on a person-to-person basis. A good pastor is one who can relate well to people personally, guide them, encourage them through difficult times, and give them confidence that he is in touch with God concerning their needs. Thus a pastor's wife should not be distressed if his public appearances are not all that she thinks they should be.

A man called to be an evangelist does need a better delivery, but this usually takes time and experience. His wife can help the most by constantly holding him up in prayer and reassuring him concerning his sermons. But whether he is a good speaker or a poor speaker, God chose your husband and didn't make a mistake. God will use him unless you destroy him by tearing him down with your so-called constructive criticisms. You cannot see your husband's depths as God can, nor can you see where God is trying to lead him and how He wants to develop him, but you can help or hinder his progress. The choice lies in your tongue.

S. Don't be upset if your husband does not always take your advice. Some times a preacher will ask his wife's opinion on a situation and then do the exact opposite of what she advised. Actually at times he may really just need a sounding board, and even though he asks, he may not really need your advice. He may have already made up his mind about a course of action and is just curious about what kind of reaction he may get. Don't let it upset you that he doesn't do what you suggest, or he will cease even to mention his plan. I used to accuse my husband of asking my opinion just so he would know what *not* to do. But I have learned how he operates and don't let it bother me anymore. Occasionally he asks my opinion, actually listens, and even agrees with me. (Not often, mind you.)

T. When you and your husband disagree on how to handle a situation in your church (and this too will happen), never insist on it being handled your way. God will deal with the shepherd concerning the sheep, and sometimes God's way of doing things defies human reasoning. You may have excellent logic on your side, the most intelligent people in the world perhaps would do it your way, and your husband may seem to be a real dunderhead in

Being a Good Wife

his idea, but if God is leading him to do it differently, don't interfere. I have heard MWs say that the severest trials in their lives came because they insisted that their husband do something the way they felt best, and everything went wrong, whereas if he had done as he had planned and as God had dealt with him to do, the problem would have been solved. If your husband messes up the situation, he must give an answer to God. If you mess it up, you must accept the blame before God. It is something to think about.

It is a wonderful privilege to be a helpmate to a man of God, to discuss the work of God with him, and to give your opinion, but to insist on your way when he does not agree is a grave mistake. Remember the trouble Aaron and Miriam got into when they decided that they knew as much as Moses? Your husband may not be a never-failing genius in your eyes, but God chose him to lead you and the church, so be very careful that you don't usurp that authority even in private.

U. The following is very important, so please read it carefully: There may be times when your husband feels that the whole world is against him, and it could be that the majority within his own personal world are indeed currently opposed to him. It could also be that his own mistakes, whether in word or deed or both, have caused these awful circumstances. It could be that he ignored sound advice and stubbornly brought about his present troubles. However, now, more than ever, he needs you to stand by him. That's all. Don't try to point out where he went wrong and why. Just let him know that you have confidence in him to work it out for the best. He now needs a loyal wife much more than he needs a brilliant counsellor.

He also needs confidence in himself restored much more than he needs confidence in your ability to straighten him out. You don't have to have an answer or a suggestion for all of his problems. Just show confidence that he will find the answers and do the right thing to correct the problems. And please be mature enough not to say in words or actions, "I tried to tell you, but you wouldn't listen." Be loving enough to show confidence, not criticism.

V. Appreciate him. Men have great egos (almost as big as women), and they love to hear how great they are. But it is almost impossible to boost their self-image while flaunting how great you are. If you constantly demonstrate your intellect or spirituality and make him feel that he is in a perpetual contest for supremacy, you are not doing him any favors. If you are intelligent, as I'm sure you are, then back off and stop parading it. Let him relax in his own home without feeling that he has to continue a battle of wits, as he may have done all day at work. I am not saying "play dumb," for no doubt he is happy and proud that you have a good mind. All I am saying is don't make an issue of it constantly, or he may run off with the village idiot. (And by the way, try to develop a good sense of humor.)

Tell him often, but only sincerely, that you recognize and appreciate his good qualities, even on small matters. Be heavy on the use of *please* and *thank you*. If you tell him often enough how much you appreciate him and how terrific he is, he will take it much better when you *occasionally* have to point out that there is something about him that is just a little bit less than super.

Being a Good Wife

Many men and women have become unfaithful to their spouses simply because they wanted to be with someone who would speak to them with kindness. Not great flattering words—just kind words. How sad! Don't let someone else speak nicer and be better at boosting your husband's moods and self-image than you are.

W. Practice what he preaches. Be a living example of his standards, or he may as well not preach them, for when people see you they feel that they see what he *really* stands for.

X. Learn his goals and then support them. Work with him instead of being a weight around his neck. Even Jesus asked how two could walk together except they be agreed. You are in the same yoke; it will be much easier on both of you if you pull in the same direction. (And he is the head ox, so to speak.)

Y. It is not always easily done, but try to give your undivided attention to his sermons, even if you have heard them a thousand times. (I realize this won't always be possible if you have small children.) People will watch for your reaction. Sometimes you will be seated toward the back, and the entire congregation will turn to see what you thought of his last statement.

One evangelist's wife told me, "Everywhere we go he tells that same joke, and every time I just know that everyone has already heard it, the joke will fall flat, and I will look like a fool." And that is how you will feel sometimes. Many a wife is in total misery every time her husband gets up to preach for fear he will do or say something wrong and embarrass her half to death. If that describes you, just relax and don't worry. Let me assure you that you are absolutely right. He will sooner or later

Nitty-Gritty for Ministers' Wives

pull out a real doozy, but these mistakes will provide you with your greatest fun and laughs down the road in a few hours, weeks, months, or years—whenever *he* is ready to laugh about it. But don't laugh (if you can help it) either behind his back or to his face until he also thinks it's funny. Sometimes husbands are too humiliated to think their mistakes are funny for a while.

Why don't we take a little intermission right here, and let me tell you about some mistakes other preachers have made (without revealing any names). In describing the clouds, darkness, and awesomeness of the Flood, one preacher earnestly declared that the "runder just thoared." Another said God told Moses to take his feet off because he was on holy ground. I once heard a young, fervent preacher say that on the Day of Pentecost there came a sound as of a righty mushing wind. My husband once preached that when David ran toward Goliath he said, "Silver and gold have I none." One preacher dramatically declared that when Peter denied the Lord the third time "the crow croaked." One man preached a stirring message, then gave the altar call and began singing, "The devil is converted and I am deserted." A lady pastor once solemnly proclaimed, "Let God be a liar and every man true."

One of our good friends once preached his heart out trying to get a certain lady to quit stalling and give her heart to God. He had been dealing with her for some time, so on this particular night, he looked right at her and said, "How about it, so-and-so; wouldn't you like to receive the Goly Host tonight?" The poor lady didn't know whether to laugh or cry. The congregation was stifling laughs, which irritated the preacher because he didn't know what

Being a Good Wife

was wrong. He repeated his invitation: "Well, do you want the Goly Host or not?" By this time everyone was in misery, and he was getting more and more upset, so he kept on till he had asked her five times to give her heart to God and receive the Goly Host. She didn't, and his wife nearly lost hers.

Some have said much worse, but their mistakes can't be printed here. Missionaries have really made some blunders while struggling with new languages. One repeatedly asked his people to please stand and cry until he learned that he was not using the right word for "pray." My husband warned the people that unless they repented God would go on a fast, which just doesn't carry the same punch as saying God will judge.

Preachers have fallen off chairs, and platforms, had their shoes fly off, been trapped in folding chairs, and had their false teeth fall out, all while preaching. So far, all the wives have survived.

Z. If you don't have it yet, ask God to give you confidence in your husband. You will know all of his faults and shortcomings. Satan will try to convince you that your husband is not all that he should be in order to make you become a stumbling block to your husband's ministry. And if you don't have confidence in him, that is exactly what you will be.

He may at times seem too hard according to your tender heart and sensitive female conscience, but remember that God chose him. If his grammar or vocabulary is not as good as yours, God still chose him. If his jokes are corny, God still chose him. Perhaps you would not have chosen him to be minister because of his many imperfections, but God did. If you don't believe in him and trust him enough to follow his lead, how can he have faith and confidence that anyone else will believe in him?

A-Z in a nutshell: Love him, take care of him, and follow him to the ends of the earth if that is where he says God has called him.

Specific Questions

Once again let us turn to some specific situations.

Should a MW resent church members for taking too much of her husband's time?

Under certain circumstances and at certain times some resentment is normal and you would be abnormal not to feel it. (For instance, when an intrusion upon his time is not at all important.) But you must realize that serving people is his calling and his job and that people will spend an eternity in heaven or hell depending on how well he does his job. With much prayer and patience, your resentment will turn to acceptance or mere disappointment.

You must adjust to the fact that your desires (not your needs) will always be second priority to his work for the Lord. However, pastors can also learn to handle interruptions more quickly or set up regular counselling hours to minimize the time members are allowed to take—except for urgent matters, which must be dealt with whenever they occur. You should deal with resentment quickly, or it will turn to bitterness and ruin your life and your husband's ministry.

How does a MW handle jealousy over her husband and

Being a Good Wife

a female church member?

First, you must honestly determine if you are overly suspicious and are jealous without reason, or if your husband is actually not careful enough in his attention to other ladies. If the former is the case, you are probably selfish with his time and attention. Prayer, time, and (if possible) counsel with a godly, experienced pastor's wife will help you to overcome your jealous spirit.

However, if your feelings are due to his lack of caution and wisdom, carefully choose a proper time and mood, then honestly confide in him about your hurt and concern over the attention that he is paying to someone else. He may not be aware of how his actions appear to others and the bad light they throw on his own ministry.

But never attack him with accusations. If he is truly being tempted by the enemy of his soul, and you throw a fit and accuse him of flirting, you may only succeed in making him angry and putting him on the defensive. If he gets stubborn over the situation, he may decide to teach you that you can't tell him what to do.

Just let him know that you are hurt, not angry, and he will be more inclined to stop. Then try your best to be understanding, supportive, and loving enough to help him through this crisis. His soul as well as others could be at stake, and a big scene with ugly accusations may drive him over the brink.

This is one situation that must be handled with extreme care and much prayer in spite of your own pain. Just as Satan tempts members and minister's wives, he may also try to tempt a minister. A temptation does not mean that your husband does not love you. Help him through this fiery trial by fighting the evil spirit behind the matter with prayer, fasting, and love for him, but don't fight against him.

Should the wife accompany the pastor to all meetings outside their own church? What about the children?

If the occasion is to include ladies, and your husband would like for you to be with him, you should make every effort to go as often as circumstances permit, not just when it is perfectly convenient. But it is not necessary to attend business sessions or all meetings outside the section.

Circumstances vary a great deal when children are involved. Very young or school-age children should not be kept out every night. While baby-sitters can be used occasionally, children should not be left with them continually. When your children cannot go, you sense that they need you, and your husband agrees, then stay home with them, and do not let anyone cause you to feel guilty.

Should a MW ever privately contradict her husband's advice to a member if she feels her advice would be more appropriate?

Never. Even if you are right, you would be wrong to cause a member to lose confidence in his counsel. Never speak critically of your husband to a member, for you will cause them to lose confidence in him and in you.

Should a wife ever show anger at her husband in front of a member?

Please don't, and ask him not to do so either. Bite your tongue till later. Satan is destroying enough homes, so give your members a good example to follow.

Being a Good Wife

Should a wife ever refuse to do something her husband asks her to do when members are present?
If you and your husband don't treat each other with respect, don't expect respect from the members. If your members see you rebel against his authority, you can count on them doing likewise. If you still like him at all, don't do that to him.

Should a MW get her feelings hurt if her husband doesn't tell her everything he knows about church members?
No! When young ladies first become part of the ministry, everything seems so interesting, and they want to know everything. As time passes, however, they learn to appreciate their husbands for keeping things from them that they cannot change or help and that would just hurt and worry them. Moreover, a pastor often receives confidential communications. Some people will scarcely tell him their secret problems and would die if they thought he would tell anyone else—even his wife. Members must have absolute trust that he will not share their deepest feeling and secrets with others. However, most things are not that secret, and the wife should be of such good character and be able to keep things confidential so that he can and will share most things with her.

Should a MW criticize her husband's sermons in an effort to help?
Never! Even helpful suggestions you may want to offer from time-to-time should be given only with the utmost care and tact. And please, never do so right after he has preached and is still very vulnerable. Wait a few days or even weeks to offer suggestions. And never tell

him, "You really blew it tonight." It would be much kinder just to shoot him. If he rattles his keys or hangs on to one pant leg with a death grip, it probably bothers you more than anyone else. You can offer to hold his keys while he preaches, but do it kindly. Or if he won't be preaching very soon, you may mention that using too many glory to God's or hallelujahs distracts from his otherwise good sermons. But let me repeat, never make corrections just after or just before he preaches.

Chapter Four

Relationship with Your Children

> Not until I became a mother did I understand how much my mother had sacrificed for me; not until I became a mother did I feel how hurt my mother was when I disobeyed; not until I became a mother did I know how proud my mother was when I achieved; not until I became a mother did I realize how much my mother loves me.
> Victoria Farnsworth

I truly don't like to break this news to you, but raising children is something no one knows enough about. Many people who have no children or whose children are not yet grown may think they know all there is to know, but they will find themselves changing their mind many times as they experience the changes that take place in their own children.

Your child will be unique in many ways while at the same time just like all the others in some ways. Even if you have ten children, you must learn how to handle each one a little differently because of his or her own personality and characteristics. Some are easy going from the time they are babies, and a mere word from you is enough to correct them. Others are headstrong from the beginning, and you will have your work cut out for you to make them do anything they don't want to do.

For example, one little girl was warned repeatedly by her father not to do a certain thing, yet that was exactly what she did. The father brought her to him and asked, "Didn't I tell you many times not to do that?" "Yes, Daddy." "Didn't I tell you that if you did it I would spank you?" "Yes, Daddy." "Then, *why* did you do it?" "Well," she said, "I thought it over and decided it was worth it."

Many times children will decide that anything you may do is not enough to keep them from at least trying out a few things, and your patience and wisdom will be tried to the limits to know what to do with them. You see, there is no such thing as a natural-born mother. The truth is, we all have to learn what to do in regard to our own children. No matter how many years you were a baby sitter for others, you have only learned the physical mechanics until you have children of your own whose well-being means more to you than your own life, whose hurts make you feel as if you are dying, and whose sicknesses can terrify you as nothing else can. There will never be anyone else you want so much for and try to help so desperately, and no one else who at times can make you feel so utterly helpless.

When you become a parent, you do not cease to be a human being with feelings, failures, and hopes of your own. Your temperament, personality, and wisdom do not change the moment you give birth. You are still just a clay vessel who must now try to shape another clay vessel. True, some do seem to have more of a knack for it than others, but in spite of what the books say, the only child expert is the Creator. The closer you stick to His instruction Book, the more success you will have with your children. Unfortunately, many people have decided that doctors, professors, and psychologists know more about children than God Himself and refuse to do what He says for fear of harming their children. Do they really think humans can be more concerned for children than Jesus?

God demands that we teach our children His Word, provide for them, and treat them fairly, justly, and lovingly. He tells us not to provoke them to wrath (Ephesians 6:4), which would be the result of unfair treatment. He does not mean that we must never do anything that they don't agree with lest we make them angry. Proverbs 23:13-14 teaches, "Withhold not correction from the child: for if thou beatest him with the rod, he shall not die. Thou shalt beat him with the rod, and shalt deliver his soul from hell." The "rod" means a thin switch, not the big iron club that many picture. In Matthew 18:6 Jesus said, "But whoso shall offend one of these little ones which believe in me, it were better for him that a millstone were hanged about his neck, and that he were drowned in the depth of the sea."

Thus, while God fully intends for us to correct our children and spank them soundly but reasonably when necessary, he makes it abundantly clear that we would be better off dead than to be guilty of child abuse. But if we refuse to spank our children, we refuse to do what God has told us to do.

Proverbs 22:6 says to train children, and training involves doing. If you tell junior to pick up his toys and then allow him to leave them for you to pick up, you are not training him; you are only trying to persuade him. A child is not in training until he starts learning to do what he is told to do.

Unrestrained screaming fits and tantrums allow children to become willful and rebellious. The professors may say that you must allow junior to do what he pleases, unless you can beg him into obeying you. But God says that children should be restrained. (See I Samuel 3:13.) The word *restrain* means to hold back from action, suppress, keep under control. God's judgment came upon Eli because he did not restrain his sons from evil. Perhaps he tried to convince them with words that they shouldn't do this or that, but God was displeased because Eli did not restrain them—so displeased that He removed the family from the priesthood.

God says that the minister must keep his children in subjection, "for if a man know not how to rule his own house, how shall he take care of the church of God?" (I Timothy 3:4-5). After children grow up and leave home, we are no longer in a position to control their behavior, which is why they need such good training while they are under our supervision; but as long as they live under our roofs, in spite of their age (Eli's sons were grown men) they are to be obedient. We will answer to God if we surrender our authority and allow them to do as they please. We can and must keep our children in subjection and enforce God's Word in our homes. Ultimately, of course, God will hold them accountable for how they react to their training.

Relationship with Your Children

For instance, I was taught right from wrong when I was growing up, but I became very rebellious and as an adult I refused to go to church. I tried to justify myself by blaming my parents, because the latest books, magazines, and psychologists declared that the parents should be tarred and feathered if a child has problems adjusting in the world.

I continued in this disgusting manner for many years until I slowly began to see, as a result of my mother's prayers and the grace of the Lord, that *I* was responsible for my misery because of my own reactions to my circumstances. My thoughts, actions, and attitudes were of my own choosing. If anything needed changing, it was I. I could never change the whole world to conform to my desires, nor could I change my childhood. How much happier I became when I abandoned the experts' advice, quit blaming my parents, and started appreciating and loving them for what they did do. They did all they were physically and emotionally able to do, and what more do I have right to expect?

Later, when I came back to church, I had to come face to face with God. Even if my parents had made mistakes, He held me accountable for my sins. I had to repent of my sins, which I had known better than to commit but was justifying on the ground that they were someone else's fault. I had to confess my wrong attitudes and ask Him to forgive me for my horrible reactions and for the things I had done wrong. According to His Word, I was drawn away of my own lust and enticed, which means I had no one to blame but myself (James 1:14-15). Thank God, He forgave me, cleansed me, and gave me the peace of mind that my rebelliousness had taken from me.

Now it is my turn to be a parent, but try as I certainly do, I know only too well that I have made mistakes and cannot qualify for any awards requiring perfection. Did I yell at my son when he and his dog came across a floor I had just mopped? No indeed, I *bellowed!* But it was surprising how quickly he learned not to cross a freshly mopped floor. When my little girl ran into the road, did I set her down and patiently teach her the dangers of playing in traffic? No, I switched her legs and promised to do it again if she got out of the yard again. She also learned very quickly that playing in the road was to be avoided at all times. (I have seen parents who have to hold their children bodily and wrestle them to keep them from disobeying, which only makes both parent and child miserable for a longer period of time.)

I don't regret the spankings I gave, but I do wish I had not yelled. But if my children's stability depends on me never doing anything to displease them, then they are going to be very shaky individuals. And if their love for me depends on my being perfect, then it is going to be a very short-lived experience, because sooner or later they will see me a bit more clearly and become aware of my flaws.

In fact "sooner" has already arrived. When we were in the States for a brief time, Tracie, who was twelve, spent the night with a close friend. She came home the next day, saying, "We stayed up most of the night talking about what bad parents we have." Her remark didn't worry me too much since she was laughing and gave me a big hug and kiss when she told me. I want my children to be able to admit my flaws (preferably to themselves of course) and be able to keep loving me without having

Relationship with Your Children

to pretend that I'm an angel from heaven.

While it is our turn to rear children, my husband and I are praying, working, paying bills, showing concern for our children, and doing our best for them. We have not duplicated the mistakes of our own parents, but we have made our own, which makes it far easier to understand our own parents' problems with child-rearing. We do not always understand our children or know what is in the depths of their hearts, in spite of how hard we try.

While my daughter and I were in Brazil we spent most of our time together because of our circumstances. We are good friends and enjoyed doing things together, and she always enjoyed for me to read aloud to her. Nevertheless, she told me when she was still in Brazil that she wished she had some friends, because she got tired of being just with me. She said she didn't want me for her buddy, she wanted me for a mother. I can understand that. Occasionally, when she did have a chance to be with other girls, she wanted me to vanish, just as I wanted her to buzz off when I was trying to talk with my friends. While we love each other very much, we do not attempt to be as one, nor can I hope to supply her every emotional need. She needs and wants interaction with many other people, and she must learn to deal with the joy and problems that other relationships will bring. She returned to the United States to finish her education, but although separated by many miles, we remain very close.

Parents can never be the all-in-all for their children. They will not be the only influence that their children will ever have, nor can they be blamed for their every hang-up. For example, when I was about thirteen I was walking along a sidewalk in a residential part of town when an old man opened his door and yelled some horrible obscenities at me. I was shaken to my toes. I had never even seen him before, but his vulgarities made me feel that I was suddenly very unclean. I wondered why he chose me to spew his swill upon. I should have told my mother, who would have handled the situation very well and helped me, but I felt too dirty and didn't want anyone to know what had been said to me. That brief moment had a very bad effect on me, and for a long time I felt absolutely defiled and without one ounce of value. It was not my parents' fault that he yelled those ugly words, nor was it their fault that I chose not to confide in them. He was evil, and I was immature and foolish. All children will have varying degrees of unpleasantness to cope with that are beyond the control of their parents. Parents should not feel guilty or accept the blame for every flaw they discover in their children.

Just as one day you awoke to the surprising and perhaps painful fact that your parents weren't perfect, so you must some day acknowledge the painful fact that your children aren't perfect either. Some parents are nearly overcome with guilt when they see flaws in their children, as if that means either that they are terrible parents or that they don't love them as they should or else they wouldn't even notice their faults. Nonsense! You are mortal, and so are your children. You have to admit their problems and flaws or you will never take steps to correct them. You may not be proud of their every word and deed, but that doesn't mean you don't love them. Sometimes they will embarrass you half to death and you may be tempted to say they belong to the neighbors, but join the club, because all parents have felt that way at

Relationship with Your Children

one time or another.

About the time they stop embarrassing you, you start embarrassing them. "Mother, don't wear that dress: people will think you're crazy." "Mother, don't park here, don't wear that scarf, why did you get those glasses, don't go to the door with that on, you drive the car like an old lady," and so on. Believe me, the tables turn.

And then the tables turn back again on them. My son is now a father with three little girls. He must try to work all day to supply their necessities and then come home to fulfill everything they think he ought to be and do. Naturally, he won't make the mistakes we did because he knows all about those. Certainly not! He will make his own.

For many, the teen years and sometimes the twenties are times of inner turmoil, self-consciousness, indecision, and frustration as they wrestle with new influences, new knowledge, peer pressure, and wildly fluctuating emotions and plans. As they struggle to free themselves from the cocoon of childhood and eagerly long to soar freely as adults, some will feel that to be completely independent they must leave everything behind and reject much of what their parents are, did, and taught. As some strive to adjust as an adult, they look for someone to blame for their mixed emotions, and some will seek out friends who are equally confused.

You can help by talking to them before they reach this stage. Explain that it is normal to be frustrated and undecided about the future during the teens so that when they start feeling this way they can cope with their emotions better. They may read articles about the Mother or Father of the Year or read greeting cards on Mother's or Father's Day and become convinced that somewhere there are absolutely heavenly parents and that they got cheated by getting stuck with mere mortals. Some will refuse to tell you their feelings and hurts and then later hold it against you because you were unable to discern what was hurting them when it was so obvious to them.

The most important thing you can do for your children is to love them simply because they are who they are, not because they are the quintessence of excellence. I really do hate to keep giving bad news, but the chances are that your son will never be the President, nor your daughter, and neither may win any prizes for their beauty.

Did you ever hear of a face only a mother can love? Such faces exist! If your child happens to fit that category, love him anyway. Deep down, some parents resent a child who looks very much like a relative or in-law whom they can barely tolerate. Take another look at your child, and if you harbor this secret feeling, admit it to yourself, and then stop blaming your child for what he looks like.

Are you embarrassed by some physical abnormality or mental deficiency on the part of your child? Don't pretend to yourself that you are not if you really are. You are not a monster; some things take a while for all of us to accept and adjust to. Start working to overcome your feelings, and be thankful for your child's assets. Please, never tease your children about their imperfections so that they become self-conscious, whether they have a million giant freckles, big ears, a funny walk, or are a little dense. It won't be funny to them even though they may laugh to conceal the hurt. If they can't feel loved, accepted, and comfortable in the environment of the home, they will seek another environment.

Relationship with Your Children

When your children have characteristics that they need to work on, don't wait until you are angry to tell them that they are lazy, greedy, jealous, or whatever. Choose a time when you are both calm and when you won't be interrupted. Then discuss the problem without making them feel that you don't love or accept them. You do not need to be proud of their every word and deed in order to love them and be a good mother.

Each of us is different and will make different mistakes, but we must provide for our families what we are materially, emotionally, and spiritually able to provide. We must love our children, spend time with them, and do our best to help them to be healthy and emotionally stable.

However, there is no need to drive yourself crazy in order to supply their every whim or to worry yourself sick for fear you may be warping them. To allow them to behave like monsters for fear of damaging their innerbeings is contrary to the Word of God.

Be careful not to influence your husband to lower biblical standards for your children. Many pastors have preached high standards until their children became teens and then lowered those standards. Some ministers lower standards only for their own children while continuing to demand more from members. This is a double standard, and the members are very quick to recognize it. Others have lowered the requirements for everyone so that they can be more liberal with their own children, have less hassle in their home, and not risk losing the love of their children. No one likes to make things unnecessarily hard on anyone, especially one's own family, but the Lord is not going to change His requirements. If we try to change

His standards, we will hurt our children in the long run.

It is not always the fault of parents when adult children rebel against them (except those parents who are child abusers or willfully negligent). It is the child's choice as to how he will react to the situations, circumstances, experiences, and influences in his life. It is fruitless for parents to dwell on what they could or should have done, or to feel guilty to the grave for unintentional failures and mistakes. Who hasn't made some?

Let's try to be aware of our limitations, learn to do better from our mistakes, and correct those mistakes we still can correct. Although we will never be perfect, that is no excuse to quit learning all we can in order to minimize our mistakes. As long as we are trying in the fear of God to love, support, and be good to our children, there is no reason to feel condemned if we are not the model of perfection.

When Adam and Eve sinned and were confronted by God for their deeds, Adam's first words were, "The woman whom thou gavest to be with me, she gave me of the tree, and I did eat" (Genesis 3:12). He tried to say that it was all his Father's fault for giving him that sinful woman. Many people still try to blame Him: "Now look, Father, if you hadn't given me those parents, that childhood, or this spouse, etc., I would be a good Christian." Did it work for Adam? No. Will it work for you? No. Will it work for your children? No.

Today, when older children rebel, fingers are often pointed at the parents, but it is not necessarily their fault, just as it is not necessarily the fault of a wife when a man falls into sin, or vice versa. We may as well quit pointing fingers at who caused whom to fall. James 1:14 says, "But every man is tempted, when he is drawn away of his own lust, and enticed."

Adam and Eve were God's first children, and they backslid. We cannot blame their Father or their environment; they simply preferred to eat the forbidden fruit rather than to obey God's Word. And they produced righteous Abel and wicked Cain. The parents were the same, but each son had to make his own choice as to how he would react to what he was taught. Jacob and Esau also made very different choices. Lucifer was in a perfect environment and in constant companionship with the other angels and God Himself, yet iniquity was found in him. That iniquity came from within his own being and was his own choice. It was also the choice of the angels whether to follow him or the Lord. We certainly cannot blame the environment, the companions, or the Father. The choice belonged to each one. Under the law, when children were rebellious they were to be stoned, but today the rocks are often thrown at the parents instead.

Sometimes children will rebel during the turbulent teens and twenties. Not all do, of course, but some do. Usually, however, if they have had good, sound, Bible-based teaching and lots of love in the home, as they mature they will begin to realize that Mom and Dad are not as bad or as dumb as they had thought and will return to their earlier training, uphold the principles they were taught, and even teach them to their own children. I am so glad that I returned.

Practical Guidelines for Child-Rearing

The foundation of a building or a person is very important to the strength of the product, so I have gathered some tips from many different mothers who have learned much by trial and error. I would like to share them with you to help you avoid mistakes that some of the rest of us have made. It is my prayer that these guidelines will help you build some very strong soldiers for the Lord.

A. Build your children's lives upon the Word of God. Don't merely rely on Sunday school teachers. In Deuteronomy 6:7 the Lord explains how and when to teach children His words: (1) "when thou sittest in thine house," (2) "when thou walkest by the way," (3) "when thou liest down," and (4) "when thou risest up." He said, "Teach them diligently unto thy children."

You must first be committed to God wholeheartedly and take seriously His instructions on how to teach your children if you expect them to be obedient to His Word. Learn to do this pleasantly; don't become a preaching nag.

B. Spend pleasant times with your children. Quantity may be limited, but strive for quality. The activities you do together do not have to be elaborate; pop popcorn together, go to the library, or make homemade ice cream. You won't have time for special activities with them every day, but do what you can in order to keep a good relationship.

C. Make special occasions really special. They make wonderful memories.

D. Have good communication when your children are young, or they won't talk later. Treat them with respect. Take time on a regular basis to let them air their grievances (respectfully) concerning things in the home, without having to fear a reprimand. They often have legitimate complaints that you may never have considered. Their having freedom to discuss them with you

Relationship with Your Children

may keep a lot of resentments from building up. Take time often to talk with each child alone and without interruption.

E. If they are interested in music, do everything possible to give them music lessons, and then make them practice. This is a good means to keep them involved in church services in a way that they enjoy. However, if they have absolutely no interest and no talent, don't force them, for not everyone is musically inclined.

F. Keep your child's secrets no matter how amusing you may find them. Get in the habit of keeping their confidences. Don't betray their trust, or you may never regain it.

G. Parents should keep a united front before their children and not contradict each other. Children learn very young how to play one parent against the other. The parents should study their children and discuss them with each other. Both should be consistent in discipline, not forbidding something one day and then allowing it the next. Discipline should be reasonable but severe enough that the children won't want to have it repeated. Neither parent should always leave it to the other to say no. Some are so afraid of losing their children's love, that they wrongly leave it to their partner to forbid things.

H. When your children are small, correct them at any time and in any place they are disobedient, unless it would disturb others, in which case take them to another room or outside. However, when they are old enough to be reasoned with, don't humiliate them by scolding them in front of others. Wait until you can handle the matter in private. You do not like to be reprimanded in front of others, and neither do older children. When you do scold them don't go on and on until you rob them of all self-respect. Be thorough, but get it over as quickly as possible. It is also humiliating and demeaning to be slapped in the face; use the other end.

I. As best you can, be what you want them to be, for they will duplicate you in many unexpected ways. Don't point the way—lead the way by being their model rather than censor.

J. Don't be continually grumpy and grouchy at home and then all smiles outside. Children are great at spotting hypocrisy and inconsistency.

K. Remember how short and tiny young ones are. Don't frighten them by flying all over them with loud, angry words and overwhelming actions. Control yourself before you try to control them.

L. Praise your children for everything from using the potty-training chair to the scribbled art work on their Sunday School papers to their adult accomplishments. Praise them equally and avoid comparisons. Favoritism is more destructive than poison.

A reporter once stated to the mother of one of the Presidents of the United States, "You must be very proud of your son." To which she replied, "Yes, I am. Which one do you mean?" She was proud of all of her sons, not just the one who became President.

M. Keep even "constructive" criticism at the very minimum, if it is necessary at all. You can challenge them to try harder far easier and more effectively than you can shame them into it. Please try not to nag them with constant corrections and rebukes. They don't like it any better than a husband does. Heaven forbid that you call them names such as dummy and stupid.

Relationship with Your Children

N. Don't demand more of them than they are capable of producing. (Perhaps they took after your husband's side of the family instead of the intellectuals and scholars on yours.)

O. Let them decide what they want to be as an adult. It is especially important to remember that only God can call someone into the ministry. The ministry is not something to pass from father to son unless God so chooses. It is very dangerous to intrude into the pulpit without the call of God; it is better for a preacher's kid to dig ditches than to preach without the call of God. The Old Testament records that even kings were severely punished for intruding into and attempting to fulfill the duties of the priests.

Some children may run from the ministerial call when it is actually the will of God for them to preach. Some may feel that they can never equal their father, or perhaps they can't bear the thought of the comparisons people may make. Others may feel that they are simply inadequate to do what God is asking of them, or they may be resentful of the demands that they know will be made on their time if they enter the ministry. There could be a million different reasons, but you must not force the decision upon them. Let them work out their own decision with God unless they truly seek your counsel.

P. Don't despair if your little ones don't bloom as early as your friend's children, as long as your doctor says they are normal. How important to you now is the timing of your first step or your first words? How many people today know these facts about you and are thrilled by them? In a very short time such things fade into the background in all but the minds of the parents. When my son, John, was born, I wanted him to do everything sooner than all the local children, but in no time at all those children had vanished out of our lives, and no one, including me, can remember who did what first. These things are just not of earthshaking importance. If the kid next door can ride his tricycle before yours can, don't get discouraged.

Biographies of our greatest men show that many of them did not achieve very much until they were around forty. Some were even thought to be mentally deficient until they got in the right field and circumstance, and then they excelled far above their peers. So you see, in thirty or forty years, your little one may turn out to be a genius. Give him time.

Q. While children should be taught and even made to share, don't force them to make their prized possessions available to destructive children. I have often warned John and Tracie that so-and-so was coming over and they needed to put away whatever they didn't want torn to shreds. Sometimes just the mention of a certain child's name would almost drive them into a panic as they got things out of reach. It was usually a child being raised by an "expert" who would not control him and so deprived him of better friendships and the liberty to play with other children's good toys.

R. Have patience with growing, uncoordinated little legs and hands. Spilled milk is often the result of undeveloped hand and eye coordination, not meanness or a desire to cause Mom more work. Even the Apostle Paul acted as a child when he was a child. Don't expect a child to behave as an adult.

S. Don't laugh at or ridicule your children's fears.

Relationship with Your Children

Even teens have fears that they should be able to discuss without being ridiculed. Things that may seem foolish to one child or person can be very real and frightening to another. Treat their plans for the future with respect also.

T. If you want to have knicknacks sitting within reach of little fingers in order to train them not to play with forbidden articles, at least start with cheap, unbreakable items until they have learned. Don't expect a little one to realize the value of a vase or figurine.

U. Be extremely careful about whom you allow to baby-sit your child, whether your child is a boy or girl. Sometimes the sitter may be all right, but she may have a relative living at her house who is very strange indeed. Never take chances with your children's well-being.

V. Don't speak of your work for the Lord as though it were drudgery, or you will fill your children with the wrong attitude, and they won't want to do anything. Rather, let them know the blessings that are reaped from doing the Lord's work.

W. Pray with your children, and teach them to pray alone. It is also good to let them know when you fast in order to teach them about fasting.

X. As much as possible, keep your more important disagreements with your husband out of earshot of your children. Many homes break up today, and children often fear that their home may be next. They will hear enough of your trivial disagreements without having to witness more serious ones.

Y. Don't discuss church problems with or in front of your children. They have enough problems without taking on yours.

Sometimes, without the parents' knowledge, children

Nitty-Gritty for Ministers' Wives

will feel that they should find a solution to a problem discussed with them, and this puts them under tremendous pressure. It may happen also that, although parents discussed a certain problem in their children's presence, they never think to let them know when the problem has been satisfactorily resolved, and the children continue to worry about what may happen long after the parents have forgotten about the situation.

Z. Don't destroy your child's faith in church members by telling them about their flaws. Believe me, they will learn enough without your having to tell them. They need to feel the security that comes from feeling surrounded by good, honest, sincere people. You destroy this security if you tell them things that you don't like about someone. If you describe a bad characteristic a certain person has, it may stay in your child's mind long after the person has conquered the flaw.

AA. Never complain to children about how much trouble or expense they are, or you will cause them to feel that they are an unnecessary burden on the ones they love the most.

BB. Keep your promises as best as you can, and try not to make promises that you will not be able to keep. It is important for your children to have confidence in your word.

CC. Answer their questions, or they will seek answers elsewhere.

DD. Be courteous to them. Don't interrupt them when they are speaking or contradict them unnecessarily, and don't allow them to do that to you either.

EE. Teach them to treat elders and those in authority with respect, or don't be surprised if they are in constant

Relationship with Your Children

trouble at school and later with the police. Support those who are in authority over them. Don't be too quick to side with your children when they get in trouble. If after checking, it appears that they were treated unfairly, you must still be careful to act respectfully and not breed rebellion, resentment, or bitterness in your children.

FF. Your children should bear the consequences of their bad behavior. If you always refuse to believe they can do wrong, and if you always bail them out of trouble, you will in fact train them to continue to do wrong.

GG. Former FBI Director J. Edgar Hoover said, "Give a child what he wants when he wants it, and you have a criminal in the making."

HH. Give your children lots of affection. Hugs, kisses, and I love you's should abound in your home daily. Don't expect them to know that you love them unless you tell them and demonstrate your love freely.

Specific Questions

The following questions deal with specific, church-related situations.

Should older children be expected to work for the church such as make or sell things, pass out tracts, and clean the church?

Cooperation should be taught to every child at every age, for they too will reap according to what they sow. You should teach them that it is a privilege to work for the Lord. In fact, it is better to describe what you are doing as the Lord's work, not church work.

Your children should not be expected to do more or less work than other children in the church who are of the same age. Nor should you always give them the choice assignments, such as leading a children's choir or passing out hymnals. Give some of the members' children an equal chance to show what they can do, or they may resent your child and treat him badly because of it. Moreover, a child should not be continually forced to do a certain task that is so repelling to him as to cause resentment against the church.

Should a pastor's children date members' children from their own church?

This practice can often lead to problems. While it has sometimes led to very good results, it has often had disastrous results. For example, the pastor's son, Johnny, dates the deacon's daughter, Susie. Susie falls in love, but Johnny does not. Susie is hurt, the deacon becomes angry, and the deacon's piano playing wife feels certain that Johnny has mistreated Susie and says so to everyone who will listen. If Susie's parents are not in church, she may become so upset that she quits church. Even if the couple falls in love and marries, they will have their problems and parents will tend to take sides.

I know it is hard to believe that these problems could happen in your case, but just to be on the safe side, be cautious with this situation. In small or isolated churches there may be little choice. It is certainly better for your child to date someone in the local church than to look to the world for someone. Nevertheless, be aware of the potential problems, and be careful.

Should members be allowed to punish the pastor's children?

Relationship with Your Children

Not unless the children have been left in the member's care and directly given that responsibility by the pastor or his wife personally. Your children should never be at the mercy of any and every member who may feel that they need to be punished.

Should the pastor or his wife punish or spank a member's child at church?

Don't spank a member's child. Doing so could even lead to a lawsuit. (Some members have given permission only to become furious when their child was actually spanked.) Instead, tactfully call the child's behavior to the parents' attention. If the parents are not available or refuse to make the child behave, you can personally tell the child to stop what he is doing or have him taken somewhere else. Sometimes it is necessary to do so to protect furnishings, expensive equipment, or instruments. Try to stay calm, and use common sense and tact. You will occasionally be tempted to break the child's little skull, but this is a definite no-no.

Should a pastor's children be expected to run errands and do odd jobs for members? What about pay?

Your children are the servants of the Lord, not slaves of the members. A favor from time to time is reasonable kindness, but it should not be demanded of them any more than any other child. Be nice if you feel that you must refuse, but firm, and don't allow others to take advantage of your children. Moreover, never permit your children to do anything that would be dangerous, such as an errand that would require crossing busy streets. Depending on what the task is or how often it is done, it may not be unreasonable for the children to receive pay.

Should a pastor's children be taught that they must be an example to others?
Unfortunately, members usually have a way of letting PKs (preacher's kids) know that they are expected to be special examples for others, but don't you teach them such a thing. They are human and may become resentful of being expected to be perfect. Or they may constantly feel guilty, because they cannot possibly live up to what everyone expects of them any more than an adult can please everybody. They should be an example only to the extent that every Christian child and every member's child should be an example. Telling them that they must be a special example for the other children in the church is a good way to make them despise the other children and dread to see them.

It is far better to show them Jesus in your own life and to show them your own love for the church and the members. If you teach them to love the Lord and to be obedient in the home, as God instructs you to do, then they will be good examples without being told that they must be. They will reflect in public what they are taught and allowed to do in the privacy of the home. Don't make their behavior a church-related issue. They should never be made to feel that other people's opinion of them is more important to you or to God than they are themselves.

If a member tells you that your child did something wrong, should you take the member's word for it and discipline your child immediately?
Under the law even criminals are innocent until

proven guilty; investigate first. Even if your child is guilty, tell the member that you will take care of it, but don't correct him until you can do it in private, provided he is old enough to wait. Tiny tots should be corrected quickly, or they won't even remember their offense.

Unfortunately, some people delight in seeing PKs catch it, but you do not need to satisfy that desire or prove that you chastise your child. If you have your child in subjection and under control at home, this will rarely be a problem at church.

Don't people sometimes tell lies on PKs?
Some sure do! Some may become angry at the pastor or his wife and try to get back at them through their children. Always check out a report about your child. Maybe it is true and maybe it is not. Moreover, it is not necessary to pass along to the child every complaint that is made about him. If it is trivial, ignore it. Remember, they too will never please everyone.

Should you believe your child if he denies guilt and then refuse to punish him?
As much as we like to believe our children would never lie, and though we may never have caught them doing so, the sad fact is that they are human. It is very likely that they may shade the truth in their own favor. Sometimes we may be at fault for expecting too much from them, and they may lie to keep us from being disappointed in them. They should never be made to feel that our love depends on their perfection. Never present yourself to them as someone who has attained such perfection that you can't understand how they may slip at times.

Check out complaints that are serious or frequent, but never judge their guilt or innocence without investigation.

For further reading on understanding and rearing children, I recommend the books of Dr. James Dobson, particularly *Hide and Seek*.

Chapter Five

Homemaking and Hospitality

Wouldn't it be wonderful if we were all perfect, could keep a spotless house, could serve perfect meals, and could be the perfect hostess, decorator, and mother? However, most of us fall short in some of these categories. Our degree of perfection is affected by our available time, money, education, and health, the number and health of our children, and our personal oomph. But failure to attain perfection should not prevent us from doing our best to keep our home at least sanitary in spite of the spots. A home should be a place where the family can relax and enjoy life.

If your home is full of love and friendliness, visitors won't be concerned if your lack of time, help, or money keeps it from looking like something out of a magazine. One nice thing you can do to prepare for overnight guests is to spend at least one night on the bed they will be using when they arrive. You may discover that it has many more lumps, bumps, and sags than you thought. If possible, correct the situation before they arrive. If the room is cold, make sure that they have plenty of covers or a heater. If it is too warm try to provide a fan or at least check to make sure the window can be opened. Shortly before they arrive, check to be sure the bathroom is clean and supplied with easily available towels, washcloths, soap, toilet tissue and air freshener. Any other nice touches you may want to add will be much appreciated.

There is no excuse for filthiness or laziness. If you do everything that is possible, you do not need to worry about what is temporarily impossible. Your husband, children, and church members want to be proud of you. You can help them to have a reason to be.

Let's think about the people who live in our homes. Since we are the Lord's ambassadors in our own home, how we portray Him to our family members is very important. Except for unusual situations, it is the mother who sets the mood and climate of a home. Her disposition will determine whether the atmosphere is tense for fear of "getting Mom mad" or relaxed because Mom is easygoing and patient. If Dad is a grouch, Mom can either neutralize his influence or emphasize it. If she complains about his attitude, she merely spreads his grouchiness throughout the house. On the other hand, if she can put forth a better mood, cheer will fill the air. If she is unable to change his mood but retains her good feeling, Dad's grouchiness will be confined to his corner. Let's face it, not every minister has attained perfection, and many wives have much to cope with in order to have a peaceful home. But blessed are the peacemakers, Mom.

A home does not have to be as quiet as a funeral in order to be peaceful. It can be a regular hubbub of good

Homemaking and Hospitality

music, ringing telephones, doors opening and closing, and people laughing and talking, if that is the way the family prefers it to be. Let your home bloom with love and understanding, and freely express your family's true personality. If you try to make your home as it is "supposed" to be, you may very well smother the inhabitants and make them despise coming home. Cleanliness and cordiality are all that are necessary, providing you can control the bedlam when quiet is actually needed. If someone comes for counsel, he or she is probably already upset and will need a quiet atmosphere in which to be soothed and helped.

If your husband pastors, learn to roll with the punches. Take interruptions of carefully laid plans with as much grace as you can, for I guarantee that they will come. Your husband is not in the church business; he is in the people business. He will always be on call twenty-four hours, which puts a greater responsibility on you to keep things at home in order. Therefore, you must be able to meet these responsibilities and to carry on in his absence, keeping yourself and the children content if not deliriously happy.

Your life as a servant of God is not your own; He bought you at a terrifically high price. If you would like to feel that you are worth at least a fraction of what He paid for you, then give, give, give. Give your time, your plans, your dreams, and your husband to the Lord. Allow the Lord to use him at any time, in any way, and in any city, state, or country that He may see fit to use him. You don't even have to like it; just be willing to accept it without continually voicing your complaints. The way you handle these disappointments and explain them to your children will help determine whether they will have a good or a rebellious attitude toward the work of the Lord and toward the members of your church. If you always complain about interruptions, church work, and church members, you can be sure that your children will grow up resentful toward the church. Things will happen that you do not like, but don't voice your displeasure in front of your children. Never get so involved in the activities of the church that you don't take time to relax with and enjoy your own family.

Specific Questions

Should a MW work outside the home if it is not a necessity?

Some can manage to do so well while others cannot. If your work outside the home is at all demanding, it may rob you of the energy and patience you will need to keep a pleasant, happy, well-run home. It may cause you to become irritable as you try to juggle the duties of your job, home, and church. A job could make it very difficult for you to be involved in and do justice to the work of the Lord, which should take priority. Moreover a problem could arise concerning how much work your husband should do around the house. Chances are that you would think he should do more than he would.

If you have young children, please consider them. I have never met a child who prefers new lamps and curtains to having his mother at home with him. You would do well to consider only a part-time job if you really feel you need time out of the house. Finally consider carefully Titus 2:5, which tells women to be "keepers at home."

Homemaking and Hospitality

Make home your first priority.

How do you cope with guilt feelings when you miss important church work because your child is sick or when you leave a sick child to do important church work?

Your sick child (or an emotionally upset child) is your first God-given responsibility. You will never be involved in any church work as important as that child. Your child's need must take priority. Don't lose your child in an effort to save others.

If your husband insists that you go somewhere with him, then he must shoulder the responsibility and the consequences. Many times the father will feel that the situation is not serious and will prefer that you accompany him, and it is true that often we mothers worry far too easily. Obey your husband, for he loves the children too and wouldn't ask you to leave them if he felt that they really needed you, but don't let it make you feel guilty. Concerned, yes. Guilty, no. Remember, it is his decision.

How do you set priorities for housework, personal appearance, church activities, husband, children, and soulwinning?

The minister and his wife should work out an agreement on housework versus church work. On different days one will take priority over the other. Is company expected? Then clean and cook. Is there an emergency at the hospital? Forget the housecleaning. You must consider what is on your agenda for each day. Try to keep yourself and your home neat, but be flexible enough to do what is important to your husband on a particular day. Keep him and the children high on your list of priorities.

Nitty-Gritty for Ministers' Wives

Train yourself, for with most of us organizing our time does not come naturally. It is not easy at first, but it is well worth the effort. If you will stick with an organized schedule for at least a couple of months, you will see its value and it will become more natural. Organization itself helps to establish priorities.

For your own sense of peace of mind it really pays to take time for Bible reading and prayer every day, even if at times you can only spare a few minutes. It will help the entire rest of the day to go smoother if you will pray first and plan later. Some days, however, you will be running from the time you get out of bed, and spending a long time on your knees in prayer will be impossible. Don't feel guilty when this happens occasionally. God understands and hears prayers you carry in your heart from task to task.

To ease pressure, have a daily schedule for your routine work if possible. It is also important to make long-range plans for events that you know are coming up. Don't wait until the last possible day to start preparations but do everything possible in advance in order to leave time for unexpected occurrences.

When you waste time by constantly sleeping too late, taking too many naps, reading too long, and so on, you only add to your own problems and frustrations. You will have guilt feelings that you may try to cover by angrily blaming others for your lack of time. In such a case, do yourself a favor; get up and at it, girl.

If a group of men gather in the pastor's home, should the wife serve refreshments and then leave the room, or is she expected to stay?

Homemaking and Hospitality

Serve and leave unless you are needed and are asked to stay.

Who can a MW go to for advice, particularly spiritual counselling, when she can't talk to her husband about a problem? (Maybe he doesn't take her problem seriously, or maybe she needs advice concerning their marriage.)

It is often difficult to find a suitable person. If there is another minister's wife whom you can trust with a confidence and who is a godly woman, she would be ideal. Sometimes, if possible, it is worth the price of a long-distance phone call to counsel with a reliable person. However, not all MWs can keep a confidence, so you should select a counselor with care and prayer. If you have a truly Christian mother or other close relative who is also part of the ministry and who would not automatically tell you how right you are, then that person would be a wonderful choice. If you are in the wrong, you need someone who will tell you, in love, that you are in error and teach you how to correct your part of the problem.

Don't go to anyone, whether relative or not, who is not also part of the ministry. Especially when church problems are involved, you may unfairly burden her with problems that God has not intended for her to bear, and you may actually do her harm, hinder her faith, or cause her to lose respect for the ministry.

Don't confide in your church members, for you could severely cripple their confidence in you or your husband. Moreover, if they ever left the church, they could spread your problem everywhere. Above all, don't confide in unsaved people, no matter how close you may feel to them. They are not led by the Spirit in their own lives and cannot render sound spiritual advice. "Blessed is the man that walketh not in the counsel of the ungodly" (Psalm 1:1).

Perhaps there is a widowed pastor's wife nearby or one who, for a number of reasons, may not be with her husband and is not currently in the role of a minister's wife. This does not mean that she has forgotten all she ever knew. She may have a wealth of experience and good counsel for another MW. If she has a good spirit and is trustworthy, then she would be an excellent choice to go to for counsel. Many times former MWs are treated as if they are just as absent as their husbands. This is a tragic mistake, and a loss of a valuable asset.

You may sometimes have a lonely, isolated walk, but prayer and trust in God's grace will bring you through. Someone once said that when you have no one but Jesus, you will learn that He is all you really need. Even when you are the most lonely and troubled, He has promised never to leave you or forsake you. Hold to that promise.

Should a pastor's wife be expected to entertain evangelists who are holding services at their church? How often?

The Bible teaches hospitality. Either food or money for food should be provided at the beginning of special services. Many evangelists have not been given food or money until the end of the services and have actually gone without enough food. Sometimes weeks pass between an evangelist's engagements. He may arrive at a church short of money but not feel right about mentioning his needs. It is true that in secular employment a person is not paid until the work is performed. However, this is not

Homemaking and Hospitality

secular employment, and we are discussing a man of God who may be in need of food or money.

Common courtesy teaches that some fellowship should be extended to the evangelist, but neither the evangelist nor the pastor should impose on or take advantage of the other. Several circumstances can alter how often and how long they should spend time together. For example, does the pastor have to go to work and need to rise early? Is he elderly or ill, or does he have odd working hours? Is there sickness in his home or among his members? Are there other problems that require a lot of his attention? Pastors' duties continue even during special services, and while fellowship is wonderful, too much can be exhausting and can actually hinder the services. But never to fellowship outside the services is unfriendly and even rude unless it simply cannot be helped. Moderation in all things is the Lord's advice, and that includes fellowship.

It would be good if the pastor, who is the host, would discuss the plans for eating and having fellowship at the beginning of the meetings so that the evangelist knows what to expect. For example, if the evangelist and his family have a motor home and eat meals there, the pastor may suggest that they get together on a particular night for dinner in his home or in a restaurant. If he doesn't want to feel pressed to entertain them every night after church, he could say something like, "As much as I love fellowship after church, I must get up very early, and I need to go to bed when we get home from the services." Maybe he could get together with them during the day. Or if the pastor loves staying up late and need not rise very early in the morning, he might suggest that they stay up late after church. Whatever he and his family prefer should be made clear from the beginning.

In any case, please be hospitable and have fellowship when you can.

Chapter Six

Relationships with Members Of Your Church

> For the ability to be of service to a fellow creature, we ought to *give* thanks, not *demand* it.
> W. J. Cameron

Relationships with the members of your church can be some of your greatest joy. You can learn to love them as if they were indeed your very own family. Many times they will bless your soul and give you gifts and honors that you feel very unworthy to receive. These are the blessings and benefits of being a pastor's wife. They are innumerable, and they make the problems worth enduring.

I feel confident that you can handle your faithful people and their gifts without advice from anyone, so let's just lock them safely in our heart for a few moments and see what we can do about some of the grace-makers, tares, thorns-in-the-flesh, or troublemakers. Some of you may think you have all of them, and others may feel that you don't have any at all, but I assure you that the enemy has planted them fairly equally throughout the field. At one time or another every farmer will find his share in his crop. Some will worry you to within an inch of your life or drive you to within a fraction of sheer insanity, but with God's help you will not only survive—you will triumph.

Some congregations inspire and uplift their pastor while others are known as "preacher-eaters." The former are mostly composed of people who love their pastor, who refuse to listen when someone tries to undermine him, and who avoid dissension like the plague. The latter seem to be made up of people who seemingly delight in tearing down and destroying pastors and who listen to and repeat absolute garbage. Usually ministers don't stay long at such places; those congregations have a continuous change of pastors because no one can suit them or endure them. How very sad they are!

A wife must be willing to follow her husband wherever God leads him and to any type of church. Much can be learned even from the worst. Some pastors have been led to stay and have conquered, but it is never easy. While other pastors report great revival, these pastors give thanks that they have merely survived one more battle.

Practical Guidelines

We cannot discuss all the causes and cares of problem saints and churches, because their name is Legion, but perhaps the following tips will help you apply a little oil in order to avoid a lot of friction. Little things really do mean a lot.

Relationships with Members

A. Be willing to take suggestions from members. We are not the only ones with good ideas. If suggestions are good, accept them, brag on those who offer them, and show your appreciation for their helpfulness. Encourage the saints to become more useful members.

B. Most of our congregations have more women than men, so you will probably be the primary example for the majority of the members, and you will want to motivate and inspire them. This is more easily accomplished by pointing out *their* good qualities, ideas, and talents rather than trying to impress them with your own. We have many intelligent, educated, talented ladies among our members, and a wise leader will use and develop them to their fullest potential for the service of the Lord.

You must guard against becoming jealous if they surpass your own abilities in a certain task. You will be happier if you can instead be very proud of them.

C. Once someone has been given a position in the church, you as the MW should be careful not to overrule or undermine him or her in that position. Certainly you are free to suggest certain things, but you should never bossily declare that something is to be done your way or else. If the person after a good trial in that position proves to be inadequate, then the pastor should replace him if necessary (and try to give him another responsibility that he may be better suited to fulfill), but as long as someone is in a position, you should never disrespectfully interfere with his decisions.

This is especially true concerning the more visible positions such as Sunday school superintendent, secretary, treasurer, and so on. Be willing to take orders from them when necessary. Treat them with respect and they will be encouraged to do even better. If you usurp their authority in their appointed office and try to take charge, however, you will create rebellious, hostile attitudes, and cooperation will go to zero. The members are well aware of your position and influence without your pulling rank, so learn how to lead without being bossy.

D. Don't allow people to take advantage of you during your husband's absence and pressure you into making a decision that he would not approve. Be strong and let them know that you will change nothing without word from your husband. If you succumb to the pressure and problems result, all fingers will be pointed at you: "She said. . . ."

E. Check your motives closely, and don't let pride creep in. A look-what-I-have-accomplished attitude won't get you anywhere in the end, unless you want very long fingernails and enjoy feeding on grass like Nebuchadnezzar (Daniel 4:30-33).

F. Don't develop a superior attitude toward others. Lucifer was very high, but he fell like lightning. A haughty spirit still comes before a fall (Proverbs 16:18).

G. Be yourself and act normally. Trying to keep up a false front will make you a nervous wreck, and people will see through it eventually. Besides, who likes a phony? Be yourself, and allow others the freedom to do likewise.

H. Be encouraged by remembering and appreciating your good, solid, faithful members. Sometimes the tares draw all the attention while the good wheat grows unnoticed. Elijah was cheered by the revelation that God had seven thousand who had not bowed their knees to Baal. Let the same thought cheer you. He has even more today who faithfully and quietly do their best to please

Relationships with Members

the Lord Jesus. The vast majority of God's people are sincere and genuine, so don't let a few renegades get you down.

I. Don't leave the impression with your members that you are above doing any work that must be done. It might be beneficial during a ladies' meeting to let them know a few of your duties so that they will be more understanding of your need to be free from certain tasks. Rarely do members realize that, while they were in bed asleep, you may have been up until 2:00 a.m. with your husband while he was counselling a young married couple who were about to split up, or in the hospital because of an emergency, or returning from an out-of-town preaching engagement.

I once worked myself nearly to a breakdown before an older, wise MW told me to explain to my ladies that I had too many other responsibilities to continue to help them clean houses and apartments, which we were doing to raise money for the church. I was afraid that they would think I was lazy or shirking my duty, but their response was, "Oh, Sister Markham, why didn't you tell us before now? We can do this without you." Talk about a relief! And God bless those ladies.

Your members don't know your schedule and duties and cannot read your mind. If you are too busy, let them know. But if yours is a small church and you are not particularly busy, then help out. I never was particularly crazy about cleaning bathrooms, but since I want every part of God's house to leave a good impression to all who come, I can't be too good to do it. In larger churches this won't be necessary for you to do, but in smaller ones, you may find that if you don't do it, it just won't get done.

If you get too good to do the unpleasant chores, don't expect the Lord to seek you out for the more prestigious tasks. Do even the most menial tasks as unto the One who lowered Himself and took on the form of a servant with no reputation in order to save your soul.

J. Keep your seat during services. Don't forever run in and out, or others will soon do likewise. Leave your seat only when it is absolutely necessary.

K. Guard your husband's time. Members will sometimes call you or your husband for the most trivial reasons. They may only want a number that is listed in the telephone book. If your husband is eating, studying, busy, or resting, it is perfectly in order to ask the nature of the call. If the call is not urgent, tell them that he will return the call as soon as he is free to do so. Don't interrupt him for every little thing, but be courteous to the caller when you must to refuse to disturb him.

L. Don't chew gum in public.

M. Keep your young children with you during service, and don't allow your teens to constantly run in and out, either during your home services or conferences. It is fun for them but very distracting to others, and they will get nothing from the service by trotting up and down aisles. Know where they are.

N. Don't hesitate to have members help you with food preparation for an evangelist or special speaker. It should be a privilege for your ladies to help. However, don't be resentful if some refuse to help; the Lord will bless you for your labors.

O. If you have a former MW in your congregation with a good spirit and attitude, allow her to share her training and experience. Perhaps she can teach a ladies'

Relationships with Members

group or the teen girls, or maybe she can speak in a special service or seminar for the area pastors' wives. She may have good ideas, but she may feel out of place to offer them unless she is asked. Many former MWs are just shuffled off to the nursery, and real treasures are buried.

P. Be without partiality toward your members and also the visitors. Even a visitor who has obviously been drinking but is not disorderly should be treated with kindness and courtesy. Many people have arrived full of beer and left full of God's new wine.

Q. Be kind and courteous to people in public places at all times, even when you are rushed or inconvenienced. It is possible that the salesperson you withered with your scornful glare or tongue may visit your church next week. As soon as she sees you she will be quick to decide that she doesn't care for your brand of Christianity. There is never an excuse for unkindness.

Speaking of kindness, please don't point out people's physical differences to them, especially in front of others. Anyone with protruding teeth, giant ears, a big nose, a bad complexion, or bowed legs, or anyone who is too fat, too skinny, too tall, or too short is no doubt already painfully aware of it and does not appreciate further comments or jokes on the subject. Making comparisons between yourself and someone else, such as, "I could make myself three dresses out of one of yours," or "I could get both my feet into one of your shoes," is cruel. These remarks may flatter the speaker, but how do they make the other person feel? She may forgive your thoughtlessness, but she probably will never forget it and will try to avoid you if you continue such hurtful remarks. As a MW you especially should let the law of kindness guide your tongue and not make jokes at another's expense.

R. Teach your people that being kind and friendly to the worst of sinners will not contaminate them or indicate that they approve of sinful habits. Some "Christians" act as though smiling at an obvious sinner will make someone think they condone the sinner's behavior. I have seen them turn their nose up at people and look down at those people while drawing robes of self-righteousness tightly about them lest they be defiled somehow—just as the Pharisees did! I shudder to think that they are supposedly representing Jesus. Did He behave like that? Are not sinners the very ones He came to seek and to save? I am not suggesting that your members partake of others' sin, but they should smile at sinners, be friendly to them, have them over for dinner, and be helpful to them when possible. Being a friend to sinners is the least they can perform in behalf of the Lord. How else will the lost be won to Him?

Once, a new neighbor moved in next to us who immediately put up a sign that read, "We are perfectly happy with our religion; thank you for not bothering us with yours." That sign bothered me and became a challenge, so one day I invited her to go shopping with me and to eat lunch at my expense. After I had her miles from home, eating food I paid for, she had little choice but to listen while I told her about the goodness of the Lord and the power of the Holy Ghost. Although she never came to the Lord, she changed many of her ideas about Pentecostals, and we became good friends as well as neighbors.

Inviting people over for a good meal or a barbeque is a good way to get them to visit your church. The Lord has never drawn people by scornful looks and haughty,

Relationships with Members

holier-than-thou attitudes, but members need to be taught this or they will think that other Christians will disapprove of them for associating with sinners. All Christians should be taught to be the friendliest people in town, especially toward visitors to the church.

S. Teach your members to be kind and friendly to people who have fallen back into sin. Many backsliders would desperately like to return to the Lord, but members of the church have been so disapproving and have thrown up such a chilly barrier that backsliders don't have the strength to penetrate it and get back in. They may eventually become too bitter even to try. The church should be a place of warmth, love, friendliness, understanding, and forgiveness if it is truly to be the house of God.

T. Be an example to your ladies in worship. Many of them will almost exactly duplicate your behavior, which means they watch you very closely, maybe more so than they realize themselves. If you want them to worship, then lead them.

U. Be faithful in church attendance, missing only when it is unavoidable, for in a large measure you will be imitated in this also.

V. According to Titus 2:4-5 young women must be taught certain things, and it will probably be your responsibility to teach them regardless of your own age. Let's examine these verses closely. The Lord wants young women to learn:

1. To be sober—temperate; not extreme or extravagant; serious; characterized by reason, sanity, self-control, and emotional balance.

2. To love their husbands. After the wedding ceremony, some young women have difficulty with this. They

must be taught how to keep love alive and well.

3. To love their children. The Lord indicates that some people need to be taught to love their children. Love for children would seem to come naturally, but some mothers resent the time, expense, and trouble children can be or even resent that their figure is no longer as pretty since the children came. Women need to be taught how to rear their children with love; perhaps some material from chapter 4 of this book would be beneficial to teach to young mothers.

4. To be discreet—careful about what one says or does; prudent; exercising sound judgment.

5. To be chaste—virtuous, decent, and modest; restrained and simple in style; not ornate; not extreme.

6. To be keepers at home. Except when there is no choice, a woman with a husband and children should spend most of her time at home in order to fulfill God's plan.

7. To be good—as it should be; suitable to a purpose; effective, efficient, and producing favorable results; beneficial; kind; virtuous; morally sound.

8. To be obedient to their own husbands. To be obedient means to submit to the orders or instructions of one in authority; to be willing to obey. If more young men were taught how to be the overseer of the home without being overbearing, young wives would have less trouble being in subjection.

At the conclusion of this list, Titus 2:5 adds, "That the word of God be not blasphemed."

W. Let your speech and actions be positive; encourage your ladies to have faith in the Lord and confidence in themselves. While it is good for them to have self-confidence, it is not good for them to brag on

Relationships with Members

themselves, their talents, their children, or their family. "Let another man praise thee, and not thine own mouth; a stranger, and not thine own lips" (Proverbs 27:2). Some will brag second hand; that is, they will tell you how great someone else said they are. For example, "Brother So-and-so said that I make the best apple pies he ever tasted" or "So-and-so said that I had the prettiest hair at the general conference." II Timothy 3:2 warns of people being lovers of themselves to the point of becoming unholy. Of course, special accomplishments and honors should be shared with those close to you but not continually for the next ten years. Proverbs 30:32 warns of acting "foolishly in lifting up thyself."

X. Be honest. If you don't know something, admit it and tell the questioner that you will try to find the answer. No one can be expected to know everything, and people will appreciate your honesty more than a possibly erroneous guess.

Y. Teach ladies with unsaved husbands to disclose his bad characteristics only to your husband or yourself and not to other members of the congregation. I have heard women testify about their husband's bad actions and attitudes, letting everyone know just how terrible it is in their home. The husband usually finds out that everyone knows what he has done, and he has no desire to show his face at church. If he gets brave enough to come anyway, many people look at him strangely and treat him as if he has the plague. (They shouldn't but some will.) If a lady really wants to win her unsaved husband's soul, she must not complain about him to the church or complain to him about the church. If situations or people are so bad at the church, why should he want to attend?

But unless you teach your ladies, some of them may continue to do this. I have known women who for years told the church all the bad things about their husbands and told their husbands all the bad things about the church or preacher; then they wonder why the Lord never brought them together.

Z. Thank God for choosing you and allowing you the privilege of helping others in their walk with the Lord. There is not another woman on earth with a more important, valuable, or significant career. The following saying puts it well:

You have been chosen by the Best
to help the best,
so do your best.

Please make time to teach your ladies. You could help them learn something in five minutes that could save them years of mistakes and heartaches.

Specific Questions

Should a PW (pastor's wife) choose one good friend in the congregation to have someone to visit and someone in whom she can confide?

No. This inevitably causes jealousy and discord among the other members. It could also bring you down in the eyes of the very one in whom you confide. It is quite natural to be drawn more to some than to others, perhaps to those you have known for years and with whom you have much in common. Nevertheless, treating them with more affection and giving them more of your time will

Relationships with Members

have a terrible effect on others. This is regrettable, but nonetheless it is true. Don't even sit with the same member too often.

How close should a PW become to members of the congregation? What about the leaders such as superintendents and youth leaders?

You should be warm and friendly to all but not intimately close to any. Jealousy is a common thing among members in regard to their pastor and his family, and you should take care not to cause it. Your own relatives are a natural exception, but you can even carry your relationship with them too far, such as by giving only them the choice positions.

If you would like to have fellowship or to entertain, invite a group or several couples at a time, making sure everyone is invited eventually. One group could be the staff, such as the Sunday school superintendent, youth leader, ladies auxiliary president, and music director. Other groups could be the adult senior class, the single young people, and the married couples. If your church is small, you could have a potluck supper in your home for everyone or split the church into two groups for separate evenings.

Should a pastor and PW be expected to visit members' homes regularly?

The answer depends on many things. In smaller churches it may be possible, but it is not with large congregations. It also depends on whether the pastor must work full-time on another job. Then there are the needs of the particular congregation. Sometimes making visits to hospitals and the sick keep a pastor too busy to visit the healthy.

If it is feasible and if you can arrange a visitation schedule, it is helpful to visit each family. You become better acquainted and know their problems better when you visit in their own home. Many times they need to discuss something but hesitate to bother you at the church or in your home. Your visits will be encouraging to them, but always let them know when you will be coming, and don't stay too long.

Should a pastor and PW have members in their home for dinner in return for each of the invitations they have accepted?

Rarely is this possible except with very small congregations. Even then you can return their kindness in other ways. Members usually love to come to the pastor's home, so some pastors have potluck meals or summer barbeques. Others have open house at Christmas and offer light refreshments; people come and go on the special day set aside for this purpose.

Should a PW baby-sit for her members? What about pay?

This responsibility should be assumed only with extreme caution if at all, except for emergencies or unusual situations. To baby-sit regularly will restrict your time, your travel, and your availability should your husband need you or should an emergency arise involving another member.

The matter of pay can be a touchy subject. Some people may not tell you but may complain to others that you charge too much or even think that you should not charge at all. Resentment can arise over discipline, injuries, and jealousy from other members (you can't keep all their kids). Then, too, baby-sitting can be difficult to drop if you find that your nerves simply can't take it. Sometimes, people simply won't pay you because you are so nice that they are sure you understand their financial situation and will be willing to wait for your money, maybe forever.

On the other hand, don't get in the habit of dropping your little darlings off on some dear, uncomplaining member. It is not fair to take advantage of her love and respect for you. You may even destroy it. Work out an agreement concerning pay in this situation also—in advance if possible.

Should a PW rebuke members?

Definitely not, not even if another PW boasts of having set someone straight. God did not give the PW that authority. Rebuking is a task reserved for the pastor. Untold bitterness, resentment and even backsliding have resulted because a wife usurped her husband's authority to rebuke and chastise. Sometimes a pastor may ask his wife to discuss something with a lady in his stead, but even this delegated role should be handled tactfully and in a courteous, godly spirit.

Is it normal for members to criticize a PW? How should she handle criticism?

It should not happen, but unfortunately it often does. All eyes watch you, and you will never please everyone. To some you are too hardhearted, while to others you are too emotional. You are either too sloppy or too prissy.

Break your neck to help a weak member, and you are playing favorites.

Such criticism is hard to take in the beginning, but eventually you will learn to do what you feel is right and not let criticism get you down.

Brace yourself, because criticism is on the way. You may be hurt to the core, but you must guard against becoming bitter over it. Pray, pray, pray.

As difficult as it is, the Lord instructs us to overcome evil with good (Romans 12:21). Moses was forbidden to enter Canaan because he reacted to the people with the same angry spirit they had displayed. When Jesus was reviled, however, He refused to revile in return.

Therefore, bite your tongue, ask for grace, and keep a Christ-like attitude and spirit. If you try to defend yourself you will probably magnify the problem, so in spite of the turmoil it may cause on the inside, keep still and pray sincerely for your critics. Jesus will give you the victory.

Sometimes members take out their resentment of a pastor's sermon on his wife or children because they are afraid to confront him. They may not really be angry at the wife personally. However, I have seen wives who asked for criticism by their snooty, hateful, or bossy attitudes. Check your attitude, manner of speaking, and spirit to make sure that people have no true reason to criticize you. If criticism constantly comes from the same source, ask for your husband's help. Don't get him stirred up and angry about the situation, however, because he must also be able to handle it with the right spirit.

Should a PW be expected to drop her own work to help

a member who calls, if it is not an emergency?

No, definitely not, unless the matter is truly urgent. Some people will take advantage of your kindness. If they learn that you will drop what you are doing at their bidding, you will be at the beck and call of everyone. Of course, if you are not busy and it wouldn't inconvenience you too much, it is always nice to lend a helping hand. But don't be afraid to refuse if you are busy, and don't feel guilty because you did refuse. Be kind and polite in your refusal, however.

How does a PW handle members who constantly rebel and refuse to help when asked to do something? Is it proper to stop asking them to help although they then complain about being left out?

You may try approaching such people with a choice of several jobs that they are capable of doing. If they continually refuse, then ask them in a tactful, kind way to let you know when they feel well enough, talented enough, or capable enough, or have time enough (whatever their hang-up is) to do something. Tell them you will be waiting to hear from them. If they still complain about being left out, then it is their problem, not yours; just ignore their complaints. Most people turn a deaf ear to the complaints of this sort of person anyway, and they won't damage your own reputation at all. Pray for them, for they are usually very unhappy individuals.

Should a PW be alone with a male church member, even if they are doing church work?

No. If you do so, you will put yourself in a potentially compromising situation. You may think nothing of it, but the man may like it entirely too much. Or an evil-minded person may learn of it and start ugly rumors. The man may have a jealous, resentful wife. Moreover, the people you least suspect sometimes tell outright lies, and he may be one of them, or someone else who sees you together may be one. In sum, don't ever be alone with another man. Ignore this warning at your own risk. You may even find that you enjoy it, which is also very dangerous.

Never fall into the satanic trap of using "I don't care what people think" as an excuse for careless behavior. According to Proverbs 22:1, "A good name is rather to be chosen than great riches." Guard your reputation carefully. A careless word, a mistake, or a foolish, impetuous action can take years to overcome. Ecclesiastes 10:1 provides a relevant warning: "Dead flies cause the ointment of the apothecary to send forth a stinking savour: so doth a little folly him that is in reputation for wisdom and honour." Don't let a little folly cause your name to stink.

What should a PW do about unnecessary, lengthy, frequent, or very early telephone calls from members?

Be kind and listen if the call is important. As soon as you have answered properly, you can very nicely excuse yourself, thank them for calling, and wish them a good day. They will soon get the idea that you are busy and don't have time for chitchat.

If your church is small you may at first have time, but as it grows you will not. If you let this practice get started, when you try to eliminate it later, the people won't understand and they could develop resentments. It is better to discourage needless phone calls in the beginning.

Concerning constant, unnecessary, very early calls, tell the callers that you are often up very late at night and ask them to please call later in the day if they need you. Of course, they should feel free to call you day or night if they have an urgent need.

Should a PW ever let one member know (through words or facial expressions) when she is angry with or dislikes another member?

No. Learn to control yourself. People will lose confidence in you, for they will know that if they ever displease you, you will do the same thing to them. Please learn to have patience with and pray for even your most disagreeable member.

Should a PW ask members not to drop in on her, or should she allow it rather than risk offending them?

If you like having people drop by, as some truly do, then install a revolving door and let them all come and go as they please. However, if constant interruptions in your busy schedule are unnerving, as it is to the majority of us, then kindly and tactfully let the members know that they are welcome any time of the day or night when there is a need but that you are not always free for unscheduled, friendly visits. Most people will readily understand this, will not be offended, and will do as you ask. However, there are a few who, no matter what you say or do, will not listen to or respect your wishes. They will continue to come to your house every time they have a few spare moments or when they are just bored. When such people constantly interrupt your work without a valid reason, you may have to greet them at the door without inviting them inside and tactfully explain that you are busy. They will eventually learn to call before coming. This should be a last resort, however.

Should a PW reveal her weaknesses to members to show them that she is just as human as they are?

If your members feel that you are only on the same level as they, why should they follow you? Shouldn't a leader at least try to be a step ahead? You are no better than they, but you should endeavor to be a little stronger in order for them to have someone they can turn to in their hour of need. If you constantly parade your weaknesses and frailties, they will be fearful of your ability to help when they need it. From time to time they will all need your support, and when people are temporarily in a weakened state they need to feel that at least their crutch is good and strong.

Let your members know that you realize you are not perfect but that you are sincerely trying to be a leader and an example. Ask them to pray for you that you can be stronger and more like Jesus. You also must continually pray for strength to bear your responsibilities, and Jesus will give you this strength. Where much is given, much is required, but it is also true that where much is required, much is given. With His strong arm to lean upon, you can do anything He or His work requires.

Should a PW counsel the members?

Only with her husband's approval. A few husbands are insecure in a few areas. Some are jealous of their wife's talents, abilities, and relationship with members and may want her to stay out of everything. You must respect your husband's feelings. Don't do anything to hurt him, make him feel inferior to you, or make him appear unnecessary.

Although you may feel that you have superior wisdom, you and your members must clearly understand that the pastor is the God-given authority over you and them. God will deal with the pastor to provide what is best for the people. The Lord can help the most insecure man to overcome his feelings of inferiority. Don't undermine your husband's authority and cause the members to turn on you. That was Absalom's undoing, and it would be yours as well.

Sometimes women find the PW much easier to talk to, and your husband may prefer that you handle some things for him, but even so you should always tell them that you have discussed the matter with him or will discuss it with him and get his advice for them. Know your own husband's attitudes, and work as closely as possible to be in agreement with his wishes. Of course, you won't need to bother him with little, everyday, trivial matters; but be careful even with these, for trivial matters, poorly handled, can grow into major problems.

Should a PW be present when her husband counsels a woman?

Joseph spent years in prison because an evil woman tempted him and became angry when she was refused. He had no witness to prove his innocence, but I have a feeling that he was never careless about being alone with another woman. There are many modern Josephs who dearly wish they had never been alone with a particular woman.

A pastor should not make pastoral visits to see women unless his wife or another person is with him. The reason is not because he cannot be trusted but to protect his own reputation and ministry. Many, many times women have deliberately told lies about a pastor and accused him of making advances or indecent suggestions. If they were alone, he has no proof that he did not. Unfortunately, many will believe such accusations, and they will put doubt in many minds. Sometimes the sweetest, most unlikely lady will do this, and therefore many people will believe her.

If a woman wishes to speak to the pastor alone, she should do so in the sanctuary in full view of everyone. If she wants more privacy, then his wife or another trusted person should be present in the room.

Sometimes while counselling, a person will ask you a very personal question about yourself. Don't feel that you must answer. You are only discussing her problem.

It is also unfortunately true that many good pastors have been led into sin by what began as an innocent encounter. Don't give the enemy the slightest occasion, or he will ruin your life. Protect your good name at all times. Remember Joseph!

Let me add that one of the most dangerous situations you can create is to allow a single woman to live in your home. Don't do this unless it is absolutely impossible to find another solution, and keep it on a very temporary basis. Many times a good-hearted man and wife have allowed a young woman to move into their home, and she has moved out with the husband or else told so many lies about him that his ministry has been destroyed. Such a

Relationships with Members

woman only has to live in the home a very short time to be able to start the lies. Such problems have even occurred with best friends and, more rarely, relatives.

A woman may be very spiritual when she moves in but may become very carnal when put into daily, close contact with a man who is kind to her. If she becomes interested in your husband and he does not return that interest, she could become very vindictive. Moreover, your husband is not made of stone, and Satan could make her look very desirable in his eyes, so be very careful lest you provide a convenient arrangement for Satan to do his worst.

Caution in this matter is not jealousy, but common sense. Unfortunately, this situation has ended disastrously time and time again and will continue to happen, with each person saying, "It won't happen to us." Although not as common, it has also happened that a single man has moved in with a pastor's family and ruined their home. I am not saying that you should never help anyone, but I am telling you to be very careful.

Should a PW ever counsel a man if he is uneasy about speaking to her husband?

The answer to the preceeding question applies to either the pastor or his wife. Don't let yourself be put or flattered into the position of counselling a man alone. Too often it is a trick of the enemy. Assure the man that he can trust your husband, and tell him that you will relay the message that he needs counsel. Make it obvious that you have no intention whatever of having an intimate conversation with him. If he persists, it is all right to be blunt with him, and by all means, tell your husband. In fact, don't keep things concerning any of the members a secret from your husband. You may withhold vital information, though it may seen trivial to you.

If a member comes to the PW and critizes the pastor for a decision or a sermon, and the wife has the same opinion as the member, should she let the member know she agrees or should she defend her husband? Should she repeat the criticism to him?

Don't make the mistake of siding with a member against your husband. You can be sure others will hear of it, and it will cause them to have less respect for you as well as your husband. Be loyal to him at all times. The best way to stop complaints about him that are made to you is to suggest that the critic discuss the matter with him. They probably won't, and the matter will be dropped. You certainly don't have to repeat every petty criticism— as a matter of fact, please don't. If ministers had a nickel for every time they were criticized, they would all be millionaires. Spare the poor fellow!

Should a PW be expected to participate in all church work projects?

Many members think so, but really you shouldn't. In a home missions work or other small church, out of necessity the PW will be involved in almost everything, but as the church grows work could and should be delegated to other capable and responsible members. She should never be domineering or act as though she alone is capable of doing things correctly. If it is not necessary for her to do the work and yet she insists on continuing, she only displays her own ignorance and inability to train

Relationships with Members

others for the job. In large churches it is simply too time consuming and frustrating to be involved in everything. In addition, others need a chance to grow, mature, and be used and blessed of God. While they should be trained to work, don't demand so much that they have no time to be with their families.

Should the PW teach Sunday school, lead the choir, and so on if others in the congregation of equal talent are available?

She and her husband should make this decision together. She should certainly have the liberty to fulfill her desire and use her talents to serve in any capacity the Lord may have qualified her for, as long as her husband is in agreement. As explained above, however, she should not feel obligated to do a particular task for which others are available and qualified. She should also be sensitive to the need to train and develop others so that they too can find fulfillment and use their talents for God.

Is it permissible to worship freely at fellowship meetings and conferences, or should the PW always behave in a dignified manner at public gatherings?

By all means, if your expression is in the Spirit and in order, worship freely wherever and however the Lord moves upon you. We would probably have much better services if more of us did so.

Can much damage really be done to a church or a husband's ministry if a PW engages in a little harmless gossip?

There is no such thing as "harmless gossip" in the

sense of talebearing. Irreparable damage can be done to the person being discussed, to the PW's own image, and to her husband's ministry. No minister wants to use another minister whose wife is a known talebearer. Please don't ever get started in this sinful practice.

Is it gossip for one MW to disclose someone's faults or sins if she is sure that the story is true, or can this be part of "knowing them that labor among you"?

It is gossip; keep your lips sealed. Perhaps the person has already repented and God has cleansed them. Jesus warned Peter not to call common or unclean anything that He has cleansed. Don't hinder anyone's future work for the Lord by keeping alive their sins, mistakes, or failures. Anyone who indulges in this type of talk will eventually kill people's confidence in them, and they usually are not liked very much. Do you like a gossip? Pointing out the weaknesses of another person won't prove that you are strong.

Proverbs 11:13 says, "A talebearer revealeth secrets: but he that is of a faithful spirit concealeth the matter." Don't you want to have a faithful spirit? According to Proverbs 25:2, "It is the glory of God to conceal a thing." Glorify God by keeping what you know of others to yourself.

If a PW cannot get the ladies' cooperation, should she ask her husband to tell them what to do from the pulpit?

If she has already tried and the ladies won't cooperate, it is preferable for the pastor to speak to them in private rather than from the pulpit. Why ruin the service for everyone else by discussing disagreeable situations that concern only a few? The PW should also check her own attitude. Many ladies will cooperate beautifully when asked in a pleasant way but will balk like a mule if bossily ordered.

However, not everyone will work, and if you try to make them, you will only become nervous and frustrated. Learn who they are, and then don't ask them.

Should a PW pray at the altar before or after church, or is it permissible to stay at the piano or organ?

Each wife should determine what is best for her, for either course of action is acceptable. Some wives are musically talented, and their husbands prefer for them to provide music while people pray. Others love to pray with others at the altar or in the prayer room. Whatever a PW chooses should be conducive to the move of the Spirit of the Lord. She and the other musicians should tune the instruments and practice before prayer time so they will not distract those who are praying. She should not allow members to involve her in unnecessary idle chitchat before the service, because her actions are instrumental in setting the mood for the service.

Perhaps the influence is unconscious, but the members will often pray or not pray depending on what they are accustomed to seeing you habitually do. They will understand when you must make an exception. Even though the majority of your time at church may be at a musical instrument, you can keep a worshipful attitude, and you should make sure that you pray before your ladies at other times in order to set a good example. For instance, be faithful to the ladies' prayer group and spend more time praying than talking. As stated earlier, the ma-

Nitty-Gritty for Ministers' Wives

jority of our congregations are women, so you will be the example to the majority of your members. Whether or not you have a prayerful church depends, to a great extent, upon you. If you can lead the ladies to pray faithfully and fervently, the men usually will also.

How does a PW keep from feeling guilty when she dislikes a particular member very much yet she must always be nice and friendly?

First, try to determine why you do not like certain people. Sometimes a person can subconsciously remind you of an unpleasant person or episode from your past, and you may dislike them without realizing why. Some people have irritating characteristics even though they are very sincere with God. Ask the Lord to give those you dislike favor in your eyes so that you can see their assets more than their liabilities. If possible, do something good for them such as taking them out to lunch or bringing them a dish when they are sick. Doing something good for a person you dislike will help you more than them.

Some people try to do right and you can love them but you cannot admire their traits and habits or feel at ease around them. You must continue to be kind, have patience with them, and pray for them to overcome the characteristics that are offensive to others. Do your tactful best to teach and guide them out of behavior that causes them to be friendless.

Some people are just too nasty for anyone to like being around, and they have no intention of changing. If, after you have made sincere efforts, they continue to be disagreeable, it is not necessary for you to keep going out of your way to spend time with them. However, never

Relationships with Members

be cruel to them, snub them, or deliberately ignore them. You must keep a good spirit no matter how bad theirs may be.

You will also probably have your share of genuine, one-hundred-percent hypocrites. Continue to be courteous and kind to them, and let your husband do whatever must be done about them.

A missionary told me about a man in his church who caused him trouble all the time and who lived a very sinful life outside the church. One night in service the Lord told the missionary to pray with that man, but he was so disgusted with him that he would not. The Lord had to speak to him three times before he finally went and laid hands on the man. When he did, the man turned and said in perfect English, a language he could not speak, "I am in him. I am not coming out, and there is nothing you can do about it."

I asked the missionary what he did next. He said, "I jumped back about three feet, and every hair on my head stood up. Then I remembered that I was a preacher of the Name and there *was* something I could do about it." He prayed for the man and the devil was cast out. The man later became a good preacher.

The Lord saw something in that man's heart in spite of his bad actions and wanted to save him. Therefore, be most careful how you treat anyone lest you make a very tragic mistake.

Should a PW dress about like her average saint, or should she always strive to be the best dressed?
The Bible teaches moderation in all things. Even if your income allows, you should never dress extravagantly.

On the other hand, dress with care and in as good taste as possible. Always try to be neat, clean, and attractive even if your members do not.

Before my husband became a minister I once overheard two PWs talking. One complimented the other on her pretty dress. The other said, "I was almost afraid to wear it because the members look at me so funny every time I get a new dress." At the time I didn't know what she meant, but I do now. A few people will resent your getting new clothes or even eating out in restaurants if they feel that their tithes have been used frivolously. Nevertheless, don't let their attitude stop you from being nicely dressed.

Dress to please the Lord and your husband, but never get into a competition to be the best dressed. Nor should you dress so elaborately that the majority of your members are truly made to feel inferior.

Repeated Messages

Sometimes my husband will preach a certain sermon, an evangelist will then preach the same thought, and the people will act as if it is the first time they have heard such a wonderful thing. Why do they do this? This is a very common occurrence and has caused more than one PW to grind her teeth to keep from slugging someone.

One PW related the following story. A member came to her praising the evangelist's wonderful message, and she replied, "But Sister So-and-so, my husband preached that very same thing in our last service." The member answered, "Oh, did he? Well, when I don't want to listen to him, I just tune him out."

I have no idea why people seemingly appreciate the

Relationships with Members

evangelist's message more, but perhaps this story explains why the Lord has messages repeated: some people have to be told something repeatedly before it finally penetrates. Try not to let a situation like this upset you.

Visitors to Your Church

Your church will never grow unless you have visitors, so it is most important that you learn how to treat visitors when they do come. You should have an intense desire to see *any* soul walk in the door, regardless of social class, financial standing, race, or age. The first thing you must realize is that if people don't have Jesus in their life they are coming to you with great needs. You are there to meet those needs and to give them confidence that they can find Jesus in your church. Get their name and address, pay them a brief, friendly visit in the near future, learn more about their home and background in order to help them and also to make them feel welcome.

If they come on Sunday morning with their children, make sure they meet their children's teacher—before class if possible. Train your teachers to be friendly and helpful and to visit the home to learn the child's needs. Don't appoint a person to teach Sunday school who has a cranky, sour disposition. If teachers are more interested in very strict discipline than in loving the children, they could do untold harm to little souls and turn them away from the Lord for life. You are better off without a Sunday school class than to have a class with an unqualified, miserable teacher. It is also important that your teachers teach stories and lessons from the Bible—not fairy tales.

Visting in the homes of your visitors will help give you a burden for their souls. If you want a burden for souls you must get out where the souls are. A burden is more than a feeling of concern; it is a heavy load to carry. It is work! If someone claims to have a heavy burden for something and is not helping to carry the workload, he is only kidding himself.

As your church grows it may be increasingly difficult for you to become personally involved with every visitor, but you can help your husband find qualified, spiritual people to do the things mentioned. Even so, keep your own heart tender, and be involved in winning souls personally every time you have a chance. Don't let the mechanics of keeping a church going cause your concern for people to run dry, or your very own soul could be in danger. Sometimes just taking care of your existing members can become a bit discouraging, but helping to win a brand-new soul to the Lord and watching them receive the Holy Ghost is the best medicine in the world for low spirits.

Teach the parents in your church not to let their children stare at visitors. Some of the little darlings will turn around on the pew right in front of strangers and never so much as blink while they stare a hole through them. This is very distracting and makes visitors feel very uncomfortable, especially if they are handicapped in some way.

Whether your visitors are other ministers or sinners, you should never leave them standing around idly to twiddle their thumbs and feel foolish, either before or after a service, while you unnecessarily visit and laugh with your members. Ministers may understand when duty keeps you occupied, but sinners may not. To neglect any visitor to the house of God while you have a good time with someone else is rude. Treat visitors to God's house with the same courtesy and kindness that you would show them if they were in your own home. If you can't be with them, ask one of your friendly, interesting members to visit with them until you can join them. But please spare them from people who are likely to ask personal, embarrassing questions.

If the visitors are also guests in your own home and you are unable to join them reasonably soon, ask your assistant pastor or a trusted lay leader to take them home or to a restaurant where you can join them when you are free. Perhaps you can send them in a taxi if that is reasonable. If posssible, don't keep guests dawdling around unnecessarily while you have a counselling session or perform some other time-consuming duty.

Many sinners enjoy a service but never come back because of lack of friendliness before or after the service. I have seen members having a wonderful time among themselves while no one so much as speaks to a visitor. Then I have seen other churches where the members greet visitors and introduce themselves, with at least one person remaining with them until the pastor, his wife, the assistant, or an appointed person can join them. If the pastor himself can join them, it is better for the other members to let them talk alone just in case the person has a need he would like to discuss with the pastor.

This kind of treatment from members comes only through teaching. Don't expect your members to do the right thing automatically unless you have taught them. Remember, if visitors to your church do not feel wanted and accepted, they are not likely to come back. Jesus suffered a cruel, painful death for every soul who walks through your doors, and He wants all of them treated in

Nitty-Gritty for Ministers' Wives

such a way that they can be more easily won to Him. Help Him, won't you?

Chapter Seven

Relationships with the Former Pastor And Neighboring Pastors

*I*f you are a new minister's wife, you may not yet be fully aware of the vital necessity of keeping a good, healthy reputation among the other ministering brethren. You and your husband's relationship with them can be a source of great blessings. You can enjoy wonderful fellowship and be uplifted, encouraged, and helped over many difficult obstacles by their helping hands. However, if you become careless and ruin your good name by betraying their trust in you or by practicing poor ministerial ethics, you can become very lonely and destroy much of the joy in your own life. Strive to be exceptionally honest and aboveboard in your associations with other ministers and their wives, and never try to convince your husband to do anything that will cause others to question his Christianity or his ethics.

Specific Questions
With these few words to the wise, let us go directly

to specific questions and answers.

Should a PW correspond with members from a church that her husband formerly pastored?
Unless the members are close relatives, it is better if you do not correspond with them. However, certain rare occasions may make it necessary; in such cases get permission from their new pastor each time. When contact is made, come quickly to the point and do not listen to church problems or criticize the new pastor. Some disreputable deeds of pastors and pastors' wives make this procedure necessary to protect you from being accused of similar actions.

Should a PW counsel another pastor's member or her former members if they contact her?
No! God is not going to deal with you concerning their problem, and in spite of your concern, you would be out of order to listen to or offer them advice. Be kind and polite, but firmly direct them back to their own pastor. Then for your own reputation's sake and the sake of your relationship with the other pastor, you should let him know that you were contacted but assure him that you did not interfere. The member may go to the pastor with an entirely different story about what you had to say, causing you many problems if he has not previously heard the truth from you.

If those who contact you are your former members, they may have changed a great deal since you left, and your advice may completely destroy what the new pastor is trying to accomplish with them. Moreover, they will rarely tell the whole story, and you will not know the spirit of the matter. You would not want a former pastor or his wife advising your members, so don't do that to anyone else and destroy your relationship with them. The new pastor has been given the oversight and the responsibility for their souls, so you must leave the matter in his hands.

For your own reputation's sake and the sake of your ministry, be kind and friendly but otherwise don't become involved with the members of another man's congregation lest you may be accused of trying to entice them into your own fold. When God sent the prophet Nathan to confront King David for his sinful behavior with Bathsheba, he did not expressly mention adultery and murder. Instead, he pointed his finger in the face of the king and said, in effect, "King or no king, you are a sheep-stealer, David." Even someone as close to God as David, was not to take someone God had not given to him. God pointed out that He had given many things to David, and he should have been content with what he had been given. We also must be content with those God has given us, for God is no respecter of persons. If He punished a king, he will just as surely punish us when we do wrong.

If the other pastor is suspected of being in sin, the presbyter and district superintendent can help the entire church much more efficiently if no one else interferes and causes the sheep to scatter. "Let all things be done decently and in order" (I Corinthians 14:40).

Should a PW ever visit the members of any of our other churches or write to them?

Only with their pastor's permission each time and only under special circumstances even then. Don't discuss their church problems and never undermine their pastor or his wife. The members need to have confidence in their pastor. If you destroy that trust you could destroy *them,* and that would be a fearful thing to have to confess to the Lord.

Your Fellow Pastor's Rebellious Members

Sometimes a man of God will enter a city, begin a church, struggle, work, pray, sacrifice and build a good, strong church, and it will be the will of God for him to stay there his entire life. That is wonderful, for even though such a church will certainly have ups and downs, it is almost always a very stable church because throughout the years it has been led by the same shepherd.

Some churches do not have this history of stability, however, and many will have several changes of pastors, perhaps through no fault of the lay members. Nevertheless, when a church goes through many pastors the situation often produces at least a few, if not many, willful and rebellious members. Some men and women who have been through several changes of pastors begin to feel that the church is their own personal work and that they outrank the pastor because they have been there longer. Sometimes it is easy to sympathize with their feelings. They have seen so many things change that they long for stability and something they can count on, and consequently they are tempted to take matters into their own hands.

This attitude is very dangerous to their own souls as well as to those they will affect. It is not the will of God for members to dictate to the pastor how things should be done or what should or should not be preached. The

Relationships with the Former Pastor

man of God has been given the oversight of the church and is accountable to God for this responsibility. How fearful it is for a lay member to usurp that God-given authority and rebel against the pastor. However, rebellion against a pastor is nothing new and will no doubt be happening when the Lord returns. Moses had lay members like that, and God caused the ground to open up and devour them. I fear that many more will be destroyed by the wrath of God for the same thing on the Day of Judgment.

When a lay member, for whatever reason, decides that he should take charge of a situation, the pastor will have his hands full in trying to keep the peace. More than one innocent pastor has been viciously maligned and attacked by rebellious members who may even go to another pastor with all sorts of wild accusations. Don't listen to members from other churches if they start telling you vile things about their pastor. Let the presbyter and the district superintendent handle the matter without your interference.

Assuming the Pastorate of a Church

Sometimes when there is a change of pastors, some members will try to pull the same trick that children try on parents. That is, they will pit one against the other. For example, they may tell you, "Brother Old Pastor always allowed us to do such-and-such, and he was such a wonderful man of God."

You are now in a dilemma. You certainly want the members to think that your husband is as wonderful as the former pastor, so do you try to convince him to allow something that he may feel is wrong? Or do you want to stand against the practice, knowing that, if you do, they will think less of him than the former man?

Bear in mind that the members are sometimes not telling the whole, unvarnished truth. Many times the former pastor was also against the practice, but they did it secretly and are now pushing to have it made "legal."

Some people may try a different approach, such as, "Brother Old Pastor was so narrow-minded that he wouldn't even allow us to do such-and-such." The implication is clear: "Either you folks let us do it, or your name is also mud."

Many times these subtle messages are not given directly to the pastor, but to his wife. Don't feel that you must reply to such remarks and tell how you or your husband stand on a particular matter. Let your husband handle this. He also should not feel obligated to make any statements at the moment. He could simply say, "I will teach on that subject soon." Then when he does, everyone will know where he stands and why; whereas, if he only tells one member, his answer may become grossly distorted by the time everyone hears about it.

Many times members will completely distort the character of the previous pastor and his wife. They may constantly tell you how marvelous they were until you wonder if they were human or incarnate angels. Some members have carried this praise to such extremes that the new pastor and his wife want to croak every time they hear the former pastor's name mentioned. Or members may go to the other extreme and talk as if you have replaced Lucifer himself.

If possible, try to get acquainted with the former pastor and wife on a personal basis before some members have a chance to make you jealous of them or despise

Relationships with the Former Pastor

them. More than likely, they were like you—mere mortals. Give the former pastor and his wife the benefit of the doubt until you can learn more about them personally. He may have pulled some pretty drastic things because they drove him to it; after you are with this particular congregation for a while, you may pull some pretty drastic stunts yourself.

You can usually get a more accurate understanding of a pastor by his reputation among other pastors, but don't judge him by what his members say. Sometimes churches are composed of one or two families including aunts, uncles, cousins, and in-laws. If a pastor crosses one of them, the whole congregation turns on him. Don't let them cause you to jump to an erroneous conclusion. Remember, 250 people complained against Pastor Moses, but they were *all* wrong. Even his own brother and sister decided he needed a few improvements, but God seemed to think Moses was doing just fine. Do yourself a favor and don't judge another pastor. He is your brother; believe in him and you will feel better.

The best thing you can do for your husband's ministry is to keep a good name and a clean record among the other ministers and their wives. Be careful that you do not cause you or your husband to lose respect in their eyes by taking up the cause of a lay member against his pastor. Leave such matters in the hands of the presbyter and district superintendent, and keep your record clean.

Belief and trust in my fellow ministers and their wives give me much strength, but I am not so naive and simple that I believe every one of them is what he or she ought to be. However, I am firmly convinced that the vast majority of them are sincere before God, even though everyone is subject to flaws. The more we have patience with our fellow ministers and their wives, are helpful to them, and refuse to hurt or undermine them in any way, the more God will be pleased and help us. In this matter, as in all others, we reap what we sow.

We must be very careful how we judge our fellow pastors and their wives, for the Lord warns us that we will be judged by the same judgment (Matthew 7:2). One time when John was a very small boy, he took his bath, and when I came in to dry him I found that he was spotlessly clean from the neck down but that his face was still untouched by water and was very dirty. Years later, Tracie did the very same thing. As I looked at her I began to laugh and said, "Tracie, one time when John was little he took a bath and got completely clean but left his face very dirty." I was about to add that she had now done the same thing, but I didn't have time, for she interrupted me and said, "Boy, I'm glad I don't do things like that!" I have often heard people say something derogatory about others, when they had left their own faces dirty.

Chapter Eight

Wives of Assistant Pastors And Missionaries on Deputation

Assistant Pastors' Wives

As an assistant pastor's wife, you should remember that you are there to assist—not to replace. Obtain a clear understanding from the pastor and his wife as to what they expect of you, and then do not exceed those bounds even if you feel frustrated by how little or how much responsibility they give you. Feel free to discuss your role with them, but don't disobey them. Don't counsel with members unless you have been given explicit permission to do so.

Do everything possible to uplift and encourage the pastor and his wife and to hold them up in the eyes of the congregation. Never speak against them even when you may think they are making a mistake. Sometimes when you think they are wrong, they may be aware of facts that you do not possess. Many times a pastor and his wife are not at liberty to discuss with you intimate facts regarding another person, so trust them, back them, and pray for them. Pray that you will be sensitive to their needs, both spiritually and physically, for you are actually there to hold up their hands.

If a situation arises in which you find yourself totally opposed to them you still are not at liberty to act against them. If you cannot work in harmony with the pastor's programs or standards, you should discuss the problem with your husband. If he agrees, the two of you should go to the pastor to discuss and try to resolve the problem. Your husband and the pastor may agree that it would be better for the two of you to move and attend a church where you could support the pastor fully. Under no circumstances should you discuss your differences with the members, because you would not want to cause division among the flock. If the problem is a question of sin the district superintendent should handle the matter.

Wives of Missionaries on Deputation

If it is ever your good fortune to be called to the foreign field, all the advice about helping with the cooking and the cleaning of dishes, counselling without permission, receiving gifts and money from members without the pastor's knowledge and controlling your children is as true for missionary wives as for evangelists' wives. (See chapter 9.) You should never abuse the hospitality given in the homes of pastors. Let us discuss this subject in a little more detail.

A missionary wife is in a different home almost every night of the week. She has never met the majority of her

Wives of Assistant Pastors

hosts, and she will have very little time to become acquainted. It is impossible for her to know what is expected of her in every home. Some PWs may resent her for not helping them, while others may feel self-conscious working in her presence and would prefer that she stay in another room. A missionary wife should definitely offer to help with whatever needs to be done and make her willingness known. At the same time, she should not be insistent and pushy when the offer is declined unless she is a good friend of the PW.

Many PWs are ill at ease having people in their home whom they may have never seen. It is a great art to go into a home and help the PW to relax and feel comfortable with visitors in her home. The visitor will feel more comfortable as well.

Let me tell you one of my own experiences with a visiting missionary when we were pastoring in California. We had not been pastoring very long and had never had a missionary to visit, so I didn't know what to expect. One day my husband told me that Brother and Sister E. L. Freeman would be coming soon. I nearly died on the spot. To me they weren't just missionaries, they were *the* missionaries. Our church was small, and we lived in an old house more than seventy years old in the middle of a vineyard. The curtains blew even when the windows were shut, and it was impossible to keep the dust out as the fields around us were constantly being plowed. The linoleum was worn out, and the doors all hung crooked.

What would the Freemans think? What could I feed them? I was very scared until they walked in and she hugged my neck like a long-lost friend, started talking about what a pleasant, homey place I had, and began admiring my newly home-canned peaches. (Bless her, they were my pride and joy.) In no time at all she had *me* feeling at home and feeling very fortunate to be living in an old farmhouse that was falling apart.

During dinner two horrors took place, but because of the Freemans' tremendous spirits and attitudes, we were all able to laugh about them. The first was a hostess's nightmare come true. I spotted a hair going in one side of Brother Freeman's chicken ball and coming out the other. I absolutely froze. All time stood still for me as I tried to decide whether to tell him or just hope he somehow wouldn't notice. My conscience got the better of me and I told him, but he refused to allow me to replace it. We had a tug of war trying to pull it out while everybody had a good laugh. I laughed to keep from crying. Then our son, John, moved a tea pitcher a little too much and knocked my husband's full glass of tea into his lap and all over his suit. The Freemans' uproarious laughter saved the day and possibly John's life.

In spite of their sweet attitudes, however, I would have preferred to die than have Sister Freeman help me in the kitchen and see all the dumb ways I do things. Just in case someone feels the way I do, I never insist on helping when the wife says no. I always offer at least once and possibly twice, but never more than twice.

A missionary may only be in a home for one night, but the PW may have fit them into an already very busy schedule. She may already be near exhaustion before they arrive and would very much appreciate any help she could get. Both wives should consider the other. If the PW has had a light schedule and the missionary has traveled many, many hours to reach the town, the PW may want to give her a chance to relax and refresh herself before

Wives of Assistant Pastors

the service.

Once when we were on deputation, we had traveled until two a.m. to reach one town in order to be there in time for Sunday school. Soon after, we had to leave in order to reach the next town for the evening service, which meant another very long trip. When we arrived at the pastor's home, his wife opened the door. The first thing she said was, "You look worn out. Go straight to bed and we will eat after service tonight." We were marched right to the bedroom without sitting down, and we slept until she woke us to get dressed for service. She gave us some apples and cheese to eat until after service. We especially appreciated the chance to rest, because it was necessary to leave the same night in order to reach our next destination in time. However, some days we were in the same city, only in different churches, and so we had plenty of time to rest before arriving at a pastor's home.

Each lady should be helpful and considerate of the other, but a missionary should never take advantage of a PW or abuse her hospitality.

While it is true that MKs (missionary kids) usually become "hyper" from being shut up in a car for the biggest part of every day, the missionary wife still should not permit her children to be unruly or destructive in a pastor's home. Their reputations travel faster than you do.

On the other hand, it would be most helpful to the children if more pastors understood that MKs on deputation are living under very abnormal conditions and, if possible, would allow them to stay in a nursery or playroom during the service to give them a chance to unwind a little. When we were pastoring we sometimes

Nitty-Gritty for Ministers' Wives

allowed our son, John, to keep MKs in our home while the parents were in service to give them a break from so many services in a week. It is very difficult for young children to be cooped up in a car, van, or motor home all day, to enter strange homes every day, and then to sit as quietly as adults in a service nearly every night.

Older MKs sometimes have schoolwork to do, and their parents appreciate an understanding pastor and his wife who occasionally allow them to miss a service to do some work on a stable surface that isn't bumping down the road or going around corners.

Only one pastor ever suggested that I probably wouldn't backslide if I missed one service and allowed me to miss the service in order to get some rest. God bless him!

One thing most missionary wives appreciate very much is for a PW to offer the use of her washer and dryer when time permits. Often missionaries have to scout all over a city looking for a laundromat. Some of them are very dirty, have broken-down machines, and are located in sections of town that are scary, especially late at night. In one laundromat which happened to be very clean and modern, I put all my clothes that could only be washed in cold water into one machine. I checked to make sure cold water was coming out and then left for a few minutes. When I returned and checked again, I discovered that the water had become extremely hot and ruined most of my clothes. I'm sure things of this nature have happened to every missionary somewhere along the line on deputation.

However, when a PW offers her machine, be careful not to abuse the privilege. Carry your own laundry supplies, and be sure to leave everything in the room as clean as when you came.

Chapter Nine

Evangelists' Wives

In this section I would like to talk to new ministers' wives, particularly wives who have married evangelists.

First, let me say that you have a very interesting future ahead of you. You will be the envy of most of the young girls in the churches you visit for having caught an evangelist and because you get to travel to different states and Canada, go to conferences everywhere, keep up on the latest dress styles, know which shoes, nylons, and purses are "in," know all the latest hairstyles, meet many people, and learn the latest news about everybody from here to Timbuktu. What a picture you present to them! Even some of the pastors' wives may at times wish they could take off with you after a revival as they see you drive away and leave all the problems of the church in their hands. You will make many friendships, eat good food in many nice restaurants and homes, and see God move in many wonderful ways as people are filled with His Spirit, baptized in His name, and healed during your revivals.

There is much indeed to look forward to and thank God for in the life of an evangelist's wife, and I wish you God's greatest blessings as you labor for Him. However, since this book is to prepare you and help you overcome problems, we must once again leave the bright, happy side and face a few of the difficulties. Let me again remind you that the good outweighs the bad if you keep your heart and spirit right with the Lord, and if you have or can develop a good sense of humor.

Specific Questions

Should an EW (evangelist's wife) help clean and cook in a pastor's home when staying there during special services?

Yes, by all means! She should help with the work, whether it be cooking, cleaning, or washing dishes, and especially she should wash her own laundry. It is best to get a clear understanding with the PW from the very beginning about what is expected. She should ask, "What would you like for me to do while we are here in order to be of help to you?"

Many things must be considered. Does the PW have a job outside the home? Is she elderly or ill? How many and whose children are present? Are the members providing the meals? Even if you are staying in your own motor home or trailer, you should help with food and dishes if you are eating together. Moreover, when you leave the pastor's home to go to another city, be sure that you leave your living quarters clean.

Neither the PW nor the EW should be lazy or try to take advantage of the other. While an EW should definitely help, she should not be considered as the maid. Neither is she an exalted princess to be catered to and waited upon.

To help a timid, self-conscious young EW it is helpful if the PW will kindly and tactfully let her know how she could be of most help. Some are willing to do much more if they just knew what, but they are afraid to ask.

Don't forget to get the matter of laundry settled at the very beginning. Each wife should do her own clothes, but there are also towels and bedding to be considered. Revivals have been ruined because of poor attitudes on one or the other's part, and this can't be the will of God.

Should an EW write to members of a church she has visited?

Never to an acquaintance made while having services in someone's church. Under certain circumstances, with permission from the pastor, old personal friends (not members of a church the evangelist formerly pastored) may want to correspond. But even then the EW must use wisdom, must not give advice, and must not criticize the pastor or his wife.

Should an EW counsel with members of a local church?

Not without the pastor's permission. To counsel means to give advice, and this should not be done without the pastor's knowledge. While some evangelists and their wives may consider themselves to be fountains of spiritual wisdom and have only the very best of intentions, they are still out of place to counsel another man's member unless he requests them to do so. That is the pastor's God-given responsibility; he must stand before God and give an account for that member.

The EW will rarely be given the whole story. Here is one example to illustrate how a problem can develop. A teen-age girl comes to the EW and says, "My older brother is a backslider, and he recently moved into his own apartment. Do you think it would be all right if I went there to visit him?" The well-meaning EW answers, "Why certainly, dear. He's still your brother. I am sure you love him and would like to win him back to the Lord." Later, a very angry pastor informs the EW that the brother is a drug pusher who lives with two other very disreputable men, that the pastor has told the girl to stay away from her brother's apartment and only visit with him in their parents' home, and that the girl's parents don't want her over there. "Oh," says the EW, "I didn't know that. She never said a word to me about all of that."

Exactly! That is the point. She didn't know all the facts and therefore should not have given counsel, even though it didn't seem like much. Always refer people to their own pastor, who would know more details. Just very kindly say something such as, "I would love to be able to help you, but it would be better if you discussed that with your own pastor or his wife. They love you very much, and I'm sure they can give you the answer you need." Don't be rude or unkind, but be firm and refuse even if the person is insistent.

Should an evangelist and his wife visit in the homes of a pastor's members if they are invited?

Only with the permission of the pastor or if the pastor's family is also invited. If they go without the pastor, they must be very careful not to give advice or undermine the pastor in any way.

Should an EW tell the PW what is wrong in other churches where she has been?
No. This is very poor ministerial ethics. I can think of no better way to destroy your husband's reputation and possibly his ministry than to repeat what you know about other churches. The pastor and his wife know you will gossip about them, too, and it is likely that they will not invite you to return. Some men destroy their own ministry by this practice, and they don't understand why they suddenly can't get a revival anywhere.

Tell only the good things. Let the law of kindness become your tongue, and you will be welcome everywhere.

Do evangelists and their wives need fellowship with the pastor and his wife outside the services, or is the time spent with them during the service enough?
They need friendship as much as anyone. To withhold fellowship except during services, unless extreme circumstances make this unavoidable, is inhospitable, unthoughtful, and unkind. All things should be in moderation, however. Sometimes an evangelist can wear out his welcome by keeping the pastor and his family up too late. The evangelist may be able to rest the next day, but the pastor's family members have their normal duties and need their rest. By all means the pastor and the evangelist should have fellowship, but both sides should be reasonable.

Should an EW accept money or gifts from members? Should this be reported to the pastor?

It is poor ministerial ethics to receive money or gifts from another pastor's members without his knowledge. The evangelist or his family should promptly report to the pastor any offer of gifts. Since some unethical ministers and wives have unfortunately fleeced sheep, an evangelist can cause suspicion to come on his own ministry if he accepts gifts without reporting them to the pastor. It is much better to respond to an offer by saying, "Thank you very much, but I have made a rule never to accept offerings or gifts without the pastor's knowledge. Have you spoken to him about this?"

If a member wants to give you a gift and keep it a secret from the pastor, don't accept it. Any effort to practice good ministerial ethics and keep your name above reproach among other ministers will be well worth your trouble; your good reputation is of far more value than anything someone may offer you. Be kind and courteous to members who offer gifts, for more than likely they are only trying to express their gratitude and won't mind telling the pastor.

With their busy schedule, is it normal for EWs to feel very lonely sometimes?

Yes, they will probably feel lonely many times. Often they would love to settle down, make a permanent home, and build lasting friendships, but they must follow the course the Lord has set for their husband and his ministry. They often feel isolated because of the temporary nature of their ministry. They are often among near strangers, far from loved ones, and very lonely. Any effort a PW can make to help them feel wanted, loved, appreciated, and included will be very much appreciated by EWs.

Evangelists' Wives

The children of evangelists often face loneliness too. The majority of them would prefer that regular Sunday school classes and activities are not cancelled when they are present so that they can participate in them. They would also like to participate in choirs, skits, and so on when possible. Children of evangelists constantly have to make new friends, so it would be helpful for the PW to instruct the church youth to be friendly and to introduce themselves. While everyone likes to feel included, few evangelists' children enjoy being singled out for special attention in front of large groups of strangers.

Sometimes the desire to have my own home, with a place to put pretty things, walls to decorate, my own curtains, my own kitchen, and the same bed every night, becomes almost overpowering. Am I being selfish? How should I face this feeling?

No, you are not being selfish, and you should not feel guilty for having such natural, womanly desires. That you are willing to make this sacrifice to do the work of the Lord is highly commendable.

Sister Jonathan Maki once felt this way very strongly. The Lord drew her attention to Abraham and his wandering life with flimsy, flapping tents, good and bad pastures, blowing sand and grit in the teeth, all the new wells that had to be dug, and all the moving. Yet he was actually a wealthy man and could have built a permanent home in green, well-watered pastures. After she had considered his wandering life awhile, the Lord impressed her with this thought: "He could endure all those things because he had a city in his heart."

To want the things mentioned is perfectly normal; it

only becomes selfish when a wife demands that her husband leave the field, out of the will of God, in order to satisfy her desires.

One thing that may help is to buy a home, if possible, so that you can return to it occasionally for a much needed rest. Then you can shop for pretty things along the way to decorate with when you return. It would be ideal to have a home with separate living quarters that could be rented in order to have someone on the property in your absence. A home can also be a good investment. It need not be big and fancy. It would be better to purchase it before you go on the field because your income while evangelizing may be so hard to verify that securing a loan after you begin evangelizing may be difficult.

Not everyone can purchase a home, of course. If you can't, you can adjust much better if you absolutely make up your mind that you will accept the will of God for your life, even if that does not include owning a home for many years. God will give you grace.

What should be my attitude when a pastor (or his wife) is committing sin or acts as if he has no burden for the lost?

You are not holding the revival for the pastor but actually you are laboring for the Lord Jesus, who is very concerned for His children. Do everything possible to uplift and encourage the members, who no doubt need it very much. Possibly even the pastor and wife can be helped. Who knows what they have been through to bring them to this condition? If you know for a fact that they are sinful, discuss the matter with your husband (and only him). He may want to discuss the problem with the presbyter or superintendent. And be thankful that the vast majority of pastors and their wives are dedicated, sincere Christians.

Is it true that sometimes pastors will invite an evangelist to their churches and then won't feed him and will give him very little offering?

Yes, unfortunately, it is occasionally true, although the majority will treat you very kindly. A few pastors' families manage to eat enough outside the home and rarely or never mention food to the evangelist. If the evangelist has very little money, his family will have a rough time.

If we are staying at the pastor's house and he doesn't ever offer us food, is it all right to buy food and eat it in the bedroom?

Not only is it all right, it may be necessary to keep from starving. If possible, however, eat at a restaurant and bring food into the bedroom only as a last resort.

Should we offer to share food with the pastor's family?

If the pastor's reason for not offering you food is because he can't afford it and his family is also hungry, then by all means share what you have to eat. However, he and his wife simply may not want to bother with providing meals and may not want to incur the expense. In this case, you are certainly under no obligation to feed them as they are no doubt getting enough to eat elsewhere. Fortunately, this situation rarely happens and probably will never happen to you, so don't worry about it. I haven't seen any evangelists suffering from malnutrition.

Nitty-Gritty for Ministers' Wives

Is it necessary to stay in such a place, or could we cut the revival short and leave?

Let your husband be the judge, and don't pressure him to leave. God may be dealing with someone there. Stay and do your best unless God gives your husband permission to leave.

Sometimes it is difficult to constantly readjust to different people, places, and circumstances. Do other EWs have this problem?

Yes, they do. It is not easy to live on an emotional roller coaster, and it takes a special person with a deep dedication to endure the constant ups and downs. To go from a place where you are treated like a queen to a place where you are treated like a giant pain in the neck is difficult, to say the least. It is most important that you establish your own sense of worth. You know you are not a queen, and you must be equally sure that you are not dirt under someone's feet. If some people should happen to treat you as such, they are the ones who have the problem, not you. Continue to treat them kindly in spite of their own poor attitude.

Sometimes I feel like a terrible hypocrite to smile continually even when I don't feel that there is anything to smile about. What should I do?

Join the club and keep smiling. Sometimes you will smile until your jaws ache and you fear your teeth will fall out, but a sour-faced EW never blessed anyone. It is part of your position to encourage others even when you personally are in the midst of a trial. To continue to smile when you are sad and depressed is not hypocrisy, it is dedication. Sometimes it is even a sacrifice. However, if the Lord moves on you to weep your heart out during a service, by all means follow His lead and unload yourself on Him. Then get up—and smile.

Is it all right to tell my husband how I feel when I am very low or troubled? I don't want to burden him unfairly with my unhappiness.

While you should not complain constantly, whine every time things don't go your way, or be a weight around his neck, you should definitely share your deep feelings with him and let him help you over the rough spots. Maybe there are a few things he could change if he knows how much they trouble you. He should also be able to confide his problems to you. The less important daily frustrations are best relieved by learning to laugh about them together.

How can I avoid frustration when the pastor and his wife make no preparations for our coming, even when they know about it months in advance and even when we call them close to the date of arrival? For example, they may keep us waiting in front of an empty house for hours while they do something trivial, and seemingly they just don't want to bother to meet us. (Being unavoidably detained is understandable.)

How do you avoid frustration over something like this? You don't! You will feel very frustrated, and that is perfectly O.K. But you must not become bitter about the situation or behave badly in return. Sometimes your hosts won't even have a place for you to hang your clothes, although they have known months in advance that you will be staying in their home. There are many circumstances that you are not required to like—just endure. But always keep as good a spirit as possible. Maybe the Lord is trying your spirit, but even He doesn't expect you to *like* the situation.

I can't help feeling a bit irritated when in revival after revival we are put on the couch in a living room when a private room could be made available.

I don't blame you. Having nothing else available is one thing, but when other arrangements could be made with very little inconvenience, the situation is very irritating. The couch itself, may actually be a comfortable hide-a-bed, but it is the lack of privacy that bothers most evangelists and their wives. Once in a while is not so bad, but when it happens week after week it becomes a terrific strain on the nerves. It is difficult to have tender moments with your husband or a private conversation for fear someone will have forgotten something and will come through the room again. The problem is magnified when children are on the floor around your bed. Also, you worry about becoming uncovered during the night while you sleep, and no matter how hot it is you can't kick all the covers off. Then, if you happen to become ill, everyone who comes through will see you in spite of how wretched you look.

If at all possible, the pastor should provide a private place. He certainly is not obeying the Golden Rule if he puts guests in places and circumstances where he would not like to be himself.

I believe in divine healing, but I also believe in pro-

tecting my health and seeking proper medical and dental care. How can I do so while traveling year-round?

This is difficult. As a preventive measure, you can have a yearly checkup for each family member when you are near your home base, where you know a reliable doctor. The same is true with dentists, only you should go twice a year if possible.

Because you never know what you will be eating, you each should take vitamin supplements. When possible, choose whole wheat breads, whole brown rice, and fresh vegetables and fruits, while avoiding unnecessary fats and sugars. When you must eat the wrong things, eat as little as possible. Poor food choices lead to poor health and shaky nerves.

Exercise daily, if possible, even if it means only going for a quick-paced walk. Many people prefer to eat rich foods and to sleep a lot, but if you truly want to stay healthy, you must watch your nutrition and exercise.

I, too, believe in divine healing, but eating unhealthy foods unnecessarily and expecting God to keep you healthy is like chewing on rocks and expecting God to keep you from chipping a tooth. If you do all you are able to do and still become ill, you must do whatever you can under the circumstances. But the Lord will be with you, and you can safely put your trust in Him.

If you are going to have a baby, try to schedule your services so that you will get back to your home base *before* the time for delivery. You will need to be rested physically and mentally for this great event and in the hands of people you know and trust.

I have school-age children whom I teach during the day.

How can I teach them without the cooperation of the pastor and his family?

It will be extremely difficult unless you can get them to cooperate. For the pastor's family, the revival will probably last only one or two weeks. They forget that your children have year-round revival, so they often expect you to be more relaxed about their schooling. Try to explain your situation at the very first, and ask them to help you decide the best time and place to teach your children. If you have a motor home, you can teach them there. If not, maybe you could use a Sunday school room (if the church is nearby), so that you will have less interruptions. Try to find a secluded spot, even if it is in a nearby park, so that your children won't have too many distractions.

How do I handle PWs who expect me to accompany them shopping and to various places during the day when I should be teaching my children? Many expect me to make an exception just for them, but the exceptions all add up, even though I do appreciate their offers to go with them.

This can be a problem. Try to explain to the PW how difficult it is for your children to do their schoolwork if you frequently postpone helping them. Perhaps she knows a qualified person who could tutor them in your place for a short time, although you should not make this a constant practice.

In some places the pastor and his wife love to have fellowship every night after church and often go to restaurants. I don't like to keep my children up too late when they must study the next day. How can I get them to bed earlier without offending our hosts?

Our services often last a long time, and then going to restaurants makes bedtime even later. I sympathize with you and your children. Ask the pastor or his wife to let you take your children home first (probably over the children's protests) and put them to bed. Then arrange for someone to stay with them until you return, or stay with them yourself. I know it is difficult and at times impossible, but try to get your children to bed as near the same hour and as early as you can every night.

If your whole family must stay in the living room, your children will have a greater problem getting sufficient rest. Living this way for a short time won't hurt them, but week after week and month after month on the floor or on bad beds is hard on them. Pastors should do their best to provide adequate sleeping arrangements for children as well as adults. Unfortunately, without the pastor's cooperation there isn't much you can do, except hope the next place will be more considerate.

Is it all right to ask pastors to allow my children to miss some of the church services?

Here, again, many pastors only think of the time you spend with them and forget that your family is in church almost constantly. Try to judge if the pastor is understanding. If he is, ask him if your children may miss a few nights, and explain why. If the children are old enough, it may be safe to leave them alone, but if not, maybe a reliable neighbor or acquaintance could be hired to stay with them. Most pastors know that their own children wouldn't want to be in church every night of the year, and if you ask nicely, they won't demand it of yours. However, your children need to be well-behaved and obedient so that the pastor won't be terrified at the thought of leaving them in his home or in the evangelist's quarters. Frankly there are some children that I wouldn't want left alone in my house or even with a baby-sitter for fear the house may not be there when I returned.

At times I feel that evangelizing is too hard on the children. Should I insist that my husband stop evangelizing and pastor a church instead?
No! If your husband feels he is definitely in the will of God, you would be interfering with God's plan for your family. Let your husband follow the course God is setting for him and then trust the Lord to supply sufficient grace for you and the children. Some wives have demanded that their husband stop evangelizing and then watched his ministry deteriorate as he tried to minister out of the will of God.

How can I get pastors and wives to stop ignoring my children and making them feel nonexistent?
Isn't it sad how a few adults treat children as if they were subhuman? While children should be taught to be well-behaved and respectful to adults (which, alas, many evangelists don't do), it is all right to include them in a conversation if others won't. But don't allow them to interrupt others or monopolize a conversation. For instance, if a certain town is mentioned you can turn to your child and say, "Remember that town? That is where we saw the big elephant at the zoo." Then give him a chance to say something.

How nice it is when the pastor and his family realize that your children are humans with feelings and treat

Evangelists' Wives

them accordingly. They will speak friendly, maybe tease them and make them laugh, provide a decent place for them to sleep, feed them well, allow them to miss a few of the services, and maybe even arrange a few fun things for them to do. You will never want to leave such a place.

What should I do when people start telling things in front of my child that I would rather he didn't hear?

Many times when children are present but are very quiet, adults forget all about them and are prone to discuss things that they themselves wouldn't want them to hear. When you can see that this is about to happen, quickly manage to draw attention to your child's presence in some way. You can say something like, "Bobby, have you seen their pretty white cat?"—or anything else to jog the adult into remembering that the child is present. If you see that an adult is about to speak derogatorily about someone you know, quickly say something like, "Oh, yes, Susie knows him. Remember he gave you $2.00 for your birthday?"

Unfortunately you just can't stop some people, and your children will hear far more than you would like. You must try to undo the harm as best as you can. Make sure it isn't you they hear saying unkind words.

Must my children eat everything served at someone's home?

While children should definitely be kind and respectful and never make cruel statements such as "Yuk, I don't like that junk," it is all right to tell your hostess, "I'm sorry, but Bobby has never learned to like fried okra, although I love it. Could he have another slice of tomato instead, please?" If possible, serve your child's plate and just skip the things he detests. But by all means, teach your children manners and respect, or you may as well plan on having fewer revivals.

If you have a motor home, it would be good to have several meals per week alone with your family in order to preserve a sense of family. Mealtime is usually a good opportunity for family members to share the day's events and to have a time of closeness.

In what ways can I help my children cope with the pressures they face?

The most important thing you can do for them is to maintain good communication with them. Talk to them often about how they feel, and allow them to express unhappiness, frustration or anger. (Respectfully of course—not tantrums.) Let them know that you and your husband care about and understand how they feel. That in itself will go a long way to relieve the pressure.

It is hard for your children to always be the "new kid." They must continually prove themselves and readjust to new things and people. Also, children can be very cruel, and your child may be greeted at a new church by another child who says, "You are ugly and we don't like you." Your children must feel very secure in your love and approval in order to endure such things, so make sure they feel free to confide in you about their fears and hurts. Don't belittle their fears and don't minimize their hurts. Be sympathetic and understanding or they will keep their problems to themselves. They won't have many opportunities for making close friendships, and they will need you very much.

Evangelists' Wives

How do I explain to my children about the wide variety of holiness standards? Some places seem to be as loose as a Monte Carlo gambling casino, while the next place may not allow blue tennis shoes.

The most important thing is to teach your children what you personally believe to be right and wrong, and make sure that they abide by this standard. Don't allow your children to go places or to do things that you don't approve of, regardless of what a local pastor allows. If necessary, let the pastor know kindly but firmly that you have some personal convictions that you cannot compromise. Do this in a sweet spirit, however, not in a holier-than-thou attitude. Next, teach your children that you will obey the rules of the pastor where you are, out of respect for him. If there could be a question about a certain activity, first find out what the local pastor teaches, lest you inadvertently offend someone.

What should I do when a major battle breaks out in a home where we are staying?

Stay out of it! Completely! If you are in the room where the battle takes place, take your children out of the room, perhaps for a walk. When you return, ignore the problem. Do your best to pacify your own children regarding the situation. Even if your children are not with you, you should leave the room.

If we stay in a pastor's home and my husband and I have a difference that we need to settle, what should we do?

First of all, settle the difference in private. If possible, go for a drive without the children. Sometimes you may have to settle it in your bedroom with angry whispers, flashing eyes, and wildly gesturing arms, but *do* settle it. Later your pantomime fights will be funny to you (maybe much later). Living under a strain, as you often will be, it is normal to begin speaking sharply or critically at times. Try your best to remember that the problem has resulted from strain and nervous tension and not because one of you is a beast. Try to remember that you are actually on the same side and should pull together. Resolve the problem before church time so that you won't give Satan an opportunity to ruin the service through your bad spirits.

Is it true that some pastors who live in very expensive, comfortable homes, will put evangelists in terrible living quarters?

Unfortunately, this does happen occasionally, though most pastors do the best they can for you. If a pastor is starting a home missions work and is struggling financially, it is understandable that your living quarters and food may be somewhat less than desirable, but the Lord will bless you if you will accept what is offered with a grateful heart, a good spirit, and no complaints. However, a few pastors may be just too stingy and inconsiderate to do so, and they are without excuse.

Even if a place is not fancy, it should at least be clean and safe. Evangelists have been stuck in dirty storage rooms; cold, wet basements; dusty attics; cold, deserted cabins with a hairpin for a lock; broken-down, empty houses with broken windows and no water but plenty of mice and bugs; and everything else imaginable. People who do this to God's servants will have to answer to Him for not obeying His commandments to be hospitable and to do unto others as you would have them do to you.

These types usually give miserly offerings as well and are the ones who don't provide much food. Then the same people wonder why it is so hard to get evangelists to hold revivals for them. Believe me, their reputation for unnecessarily bad accommodations travels far, wide, and fast.

At such a place you must guard against becoming bitter, although you may be justifiably upset. Be willing to endure the hardness as a good soldier of the Lord. Down the road you can laugh about the situation and thank God for bringing you though it. Do your best for the Lord and the congregation even in places like these. Fortunately, they are few.

Couldn't we avoid many sleeping and eating problems by having our own trailer or motor home?

Yes, having your own quarters helps you to avoid many unpleasant things. However, many young couples simply cannot afford them. Also, the pipes on trailers freeze during the winter in some places, there is no water in the sinks or bathroom, and heating is very expensive. Sometimes no hookups are available, so you must still make other arrangements for sleeping and eating.

Let me repeat emphatically that the inhospitable places are out of the norm. In almost all places you will be treated very kindly and fed so much that you will have a constant battle to keep your girlish figure. Don't worry about poor accommodations; just be aware that once in a while you may encounter them, and don't be upset too much if you have to take your turn.

Nitty-Gritty for Ministers' Wives

I love the Lord and enjoy evangelizing, but sometimes I dread going to service. Sometimes I feel guilty and unspiritual because I don't want to face one more altar call. Is this normal?

Yes, it is normal. At times you will become physically, mentally, and emotionally drained. This does not necessarily mean that you are in a bad condition spiritually, so you have no need to feel guilty. Usually some time off to relax and refresh yourself is all that you need. The spirit may be willing, but the flesh is weak and needs rest. Besides, being spiritual does not always mean being raring to go full speed ahead. Being spiritual means willingly and obediently following the Spirit of God when you feel like it and when you don't. Even though your mind may feel a bit numb and you can't really seem to pray as you would like, you and your husband should still pray with them at the altar in order to encourage them to pray. The Lord doesn't need you to feel fresh as a daisy in order for Him to fill someone else with His Spirit.

My husband and I have not been evangelizing very long and are not widely known, but he is dedicated and a good preacher. Yet I have seen pastors deliberately change directions or cut across pews at conferences to avoid him. Why do they do this? Frankly, it is very embarrassing.

This is one of the occupational hazards of evangelizing and one of the reasons why some give up too soon. Unless he has a widespread reputation as a good evangelist (which takes time to develop), your husband will almost always be looking for revivals, and pastors know this. Some pastors feel bad when they must refuse to book evangelists and so prefer to avoid them. This is unfortunate, and it does cause hurt feelings.

Many times a pastor has recently had an evangelist, has already asked another one to come, or is in the middle of church problems and does not know when he could use one. He may even be considering resigning his church and may not know if he will be there long enough to have another revival. There could be a million reasons why he can't use your husband, none of them a reflection on your husband's ministry. Rather than explain—and you can't blame them sometimes—some pastors will avoid evangelists. You must be rather thick-skinned to be an evangelist and not take such things personally.

Time and dedication alone make an evangelist. A well-known family name or good connections may help some to get off to a better start, but unless their ministry is fruitful they won't last long. Pastors usually won't use carnal or unfruitful evangelists more than once, no matter what their name happens to be or whose daughter they are married to. Keep praying for your husband every day and assure him of your confidence in him so that situations like these won't tear him to pieces. Getting started on the evangelistic field is difficult emotionally as well as financially. Your husband needs your patience, understanding, confidence, and willingness to endure hardships, as well as your spoken love.

Many pastors also run from missionaries, who are constantly seeking Partners in Missions. They may have a million reasons why they can't support another missionary, and none of them a reflection on a particular missionary. Conferences can be very lonely for an evangelist or missionary, as people make wide circles around him to avoid being put on the spot.

Nitty-Gritty for Ministers' Wives

Why do some people forever make comparisons, brag on certain well-known evangelists, and make us feel like we will never make it because we are not as good as someone else?

The only reason I can think of is a lack of sensitivity to the feelings of others or gross ignorance. However, don't let them convince you, because 99.99 percent of all preachers have had such nonsense said to them. The other .01 percent were out of the room when these things were said about them. However, don't retaliate by putting down another evangelist in order to enhance your own image. Let these remarks go in one ear and out the other. Keep a good spirit, and serve the Lord with all your might. We are workers together—not competitors.

I have prayed for people at the altar and heard them speak in tongues beyond a shadow of a doubt; yet when I tell the pastor, he says something like, "We'll see." Why doesn't he believe me?

Because, unfortunately, some evangelists through the years, in order to enhance their own reputation, have been a little careless in their claims about how many received the Holy Ghost in their revivals. Therefore, a wise pastor will want to know for himself in order to know how to deal with that person in the future. It would be careless for him just to assume people have the Holy Ghost when in fact they never received the Spirit. When you pray with someone and they begin to speak in other tongues, get the pastor, his wife, an assistant, or another reliable witness to hear it also. I'm sure the pastor doesn't actually doubt your word or honesty, but no one is infallible, and everyone makes mistakes at times.

My husband tells me not to talk about controversial subjects. Why not? I want people to know what I believe and stand for.

Of course you should obey the Word of God and not compromise your convictions. However, it is not necessary to wave your banner about your opinions and personal convictions. If you do, you will drastically reduce the number of churches where your husband will be invited to preach. For example, Pastor A does not allow his people to wear purple shoelaces. If he hears you say, "Some people are so stupid that they won't let their people wear purple shoelaces," you can be sure that he will not invite your husband to preach a revival for him, knowing that you might show up in purple shoelaces. Or perhaps you make an emphatic statement that anyone who has a brown couch in his home is a sinner. Every pastor with a brown couch is going to cross you off his list. If you go to a place where the pastor has a brown couch, just keep quiet and don't sit on it. Sit somewhere else and keep a good spirit.

An EW should be very careful with regard to controversial subjects. If someone raises a controversial issue, you may want to say something like, "I know some wonderful people who believe that, but I'm trying to keep my heart and mind open until I can learn more about the subject." Your husband is the preacher; let him make the public declarations that he feels are necessary.

Do all evangelists repeat their messages?

All the ones I know do, and why not? If God has given a preacher a message that many people need, why should he refuse to preach it again? Usually it will vary a bit here and there as the Lord tailors it to fit a new congregation. I'm sure the apostles repeated themselves many times. Of course, an evangelist should keep his mind and heart sensitive to the Spirit of God and preach what he feels is needful for a particular service, whether it be a new message or one he has preached in many other churches.

Sometimes a MW feels that her husband is unethical if he preaches a message that he heard someone else preach, but this too is all right if God impresses him to do so and if he gives proper credit. God told preachers to feed His sheep, but He did not say that they must come up with a never-been-tried-before recipe for every meal. If the central theme of a message is biblical, as it should be, then it is not the private property of any individual.

Sometimes when a pastor hears a message, the Holy Ghost will impress him with the need for his people to hear it also. Many pastors return home from general conferences and preach for their congregations the great messages they heard there. The Landmark Convention in Stockton, California, is truly a preachers' convention, and many ministers go there to be fed themselves and then take some of the good, healthy food back to their flocks. One time most of our congregation went to a nearby conference and heard Brother David Fuller preach a tremendous message. My husband told our members that he intended to repeat Brother Fuller's sermon in our church at least once a year, which he did, and it helped them each time. Brother David Gray once gave my husband his notes on a particular sermon so that he could preach it to our people. An old but true saying is "If it is true, it probably isn't new. And if it is new, it probably isn't true." In fact, some ministers are led into false doctrine because they try so hard to come up with something completely original.

Sometimes a man will hear a good message and then forget it for several years. When it comes to mind again, he will have forgotten if or where he has heard it preached before. It really doesn't matter. If it is good for the flock, then he should serve it to them.

However, if a minister rarely studies to learn the Word of God more perfectly and to get a thought from the Lord for his own sermons but instead only preaches what he hears from someone else or from tapes, then that is another matter entirely. He is just lazy, lacks in dedication, and needs to pray. But to repeat his own sermons and occasionally to preach a thought he heard from someone else is all right. And even though you may have heard the message many times, you should still listen attentively and respectfully. Those around you have not heard it and may desperately need what is being said.

I think I have faith; why then do I sometimes feel so vulnerable?

Except for the hand of God on your life, you are vulnerable. You lack many of the things others have to make them feel secure. Many times you travel on long, empty roads far from friends and family where there is always the possibility of accidents, sickness, and theft. Many people experience this feeling on long vacations, but for you it becomes a way of life. You will often be keenly aware of your lack of security.

Not only must you learn to commit yourself fully into the hands of the Lord and accept what He allows to come your way, but you should also prepare as much as possible for emergencies. Carry in your purse and glove compartment a card that lists your names; medical facts such as blood types, the wearing of contact lenses, and allergies to drugs; and several telephone numbers to call in case of emergency. List several numbers in case someone can't be reached right away. Keep someone informed of your schedule in case someone needs to reach you in an emergency. Carry a first-aid kit, flares, snow chains if they may be necessary, and extra water in desert areas. Don't hesitate to contact police for help of any kind regarding your safety and well-being. Check a good auto club for more safety tips. Have the best insurance coverage that you can afford.

The Bible commends the ant for preparing for the future, which indicates that we should also be prepared. Expect the best, but be well prepared for the worst. Even in emergencies, the Lord will be with you; He will be a very present help in time of trouble.

When I need a woman's counsel, to whom can I go?

The answer depends on the seriousness of your problem. If it is not earthshaking, you will probably meet many MWs who can help you. However, never confide in members lest you burden them with something not meant for them to carry. If the problem is very serious, either call a qualified person or, if possible, wait until you can talk with her in person. All MWs should be careful not to place their confidence in the wrong person.

When are the most predictable bad times, financially, for evangelists?

During holidays and conventions. Very few pastors

have revivals during these times because their members are usually busy with families or traveling. Therefore, few evangelists have any income (but many expenses) during these times. If possible, try to save ahead in order to get through these financial droughts. Some very thoughtful pastors will give love offerings to evangelists they see at conferences. God bless them!

Another reason to put a little money aside is for those times when someone cancels a revival so late that you can't schedule another in its place. Most pastors won't do this except when circumstances beyond their control make it necessary. But just in case, try to have some funds to fall back on. I realize how difficult this may be, but keep it in mind, and do what you can to save for these situations.

Are there other ways to be a blessing to a church besides preaching?

Yes, and the more sought-after evangelists do much more than preach. Talk to the pastor and make yourselves available for anything he may feel would help. Maybe he would like for you to teach a new converts class, give lessons on Sunday school wall decorations (you can pick up many ideas since you visit many churches), give a class on marriage, knock doors, teach members how to give home Bible studies, or help the music program. But study and learn your subject before you attempt to teach others. If you will do more than just what is required, you will be a real blessing to the whole church, and more than likely you will be invited to return.

The Evangelist's Reputation

In closing this chapter, let me mention two points concerning the evangelist's image and reputation. First, the more an evangelizing couple can do to build up the image of the pastor and his wife, the more effective your ministry will be. Of course, you should only say those things which you know to be true, for false flattery is lying and has never helped anyone.

Some foolish young men try to impress the congregation and exalt themselves, but they are soon gone—probably not to be invited back. An evangelist should always do what is best for the sheep, and the best thing for the sheep is to have confidence in their shepherd. He is the one who looks after them, feeds them the best that he can, and gives his life for them. Their security depends in large part on how well he can do his job. An evangelist and his wife can be a tremendous help to the sheep if they will encourage them to have confidence in their shepherd. When an evangelist leaves the impression that he has better counsel than the pastor, is a better preacher, and has more power with God, then he does the members a grave disservice in order to build his own ego and image.

Don't think for one minute that the pastor doesn't see all of this. The next time he needs an evangelist, he will look for someone who is more concerned with the sheep than with his own reputation. Always commend the pastor and encourage his people to follow his leadership. This will not only help the people, but it will also help you, for only the pastor can invite you to return!

The second tip I would like to mention is about your children. Evangelizing is very difficult for lively young children, who need lots of activities and exercise to use up their abundant energy. See to it that you don't allow them to spend this energy to dismantle the pastor's home. The reputation of uncontrolled children travels faster than news of great preaching. You may find services very hard to obtain unless you make your children behave well.

Chapter Ten

A Cloud of Witnesses

Hebrews 11 contains a long list of persecutions that many people of God suffered for their belief in the Lord. Then Hebrews 12:1-3 states, "Wherefore seeing we also are compassed about with so great a cloud of witnesses, let us lay aside every weight, and the sin which doth so easily beset us, and let us run with patience the race that is set before us, Looking unto Jesus the author and finisher of our faith; who for the joy that was set before him endured the cross, despising the shame, and is set down at the right hand of the throne of God. For consider him that endured such contradiction of sinners against himself, lest ye be wearied and faint in your minds."

What wonderful advice! We should consider what the Lord suffered for us as well as what some of His people have endured. This will help us to count our blessings rather than to imagine that we are too heavily burdened and to give up our race.

The stories of people who lived thousands of years ago sometimes have an almost unreal quality and may fail to inspire us. But when we realize that there are people today who willingly suffer for His name's sake, we have a greater desire to do and bear all He has appointed unto us.

Sister Mollie Thompson's book *Of Caesar's Household* demonstrates that not all the physical suffering of God's people happened thousands of years ago. We can only imagine the atrocities that Christians suffer in some countries this very day. They are our brothers and sisters in the Lord, and we stand in awe of their courage and dedication. We wonder if we have that kind of faith and fervently hope we never have to find out the hard way.

But what about our brothers and sisters all around us who have not had to face brutal persecution for Jesus but who would amaze even themselves if the need arose? I believe with all my heart that we have many seemingly frivolous teens who would find depths of love and dedication they haven't realized and who would be strong enough to give their very lives for Jesus if such an occasion should arise. We have lonely, elderly folks who could summon enough strength from the Holy Ghost to look death in the face and give their all if need be. We cannot see the depths of our brothers and sisters because most of our lives are free from the visible fiery furnaces, but nevertheless, those all around us are engaged in the battle for their souls every day.

How we need one another! We must hold up one another with prayer, encouraging words and deeds, and patience, especially those who fail to meet our expectations. When the apostles were in the storm on the sea, Jesus came to them and comforted them. They were amazed beyond measure because they had failed to consider the miracle of the loaves and fishes, which they had

A Cloud of Witnesses

witnessed just before getting into the boat. Mark 6:52 then adds another bit of information concerning these fantastic men of God "For their heart was hardened." Right after the tremendous experience they had enjoyed with Jesus, their heart was hardened. If these great men of God were subject to such a thing, is it not a little possible that our brothers and sisters may at times be just a little out of sorts and the tiniest bit crabby? Does this mean we should love them less? I think not. Let's have patience and longsuffering with one another. I might need a little understanding today, and you might need it tomorrow.

In II Timothy 3:1-4 we find this solemn warning: "This know also, that in the last days perilous times shall come. For men shall be lovers of their own selves . . . lovers of pleasures more than lovers of God." This particular warning is not directed against the dangers to the physical life but rather concerns the peril to the soul, which is of far greater importance. Any trap of Satan is deadly, and we should not become disgusted with someone who falls into the trap of worldly pleasure rather than the trap of physical adversity. Let us rather become alarmed, concerned, and frightened for that person's soul and make more of a loving effort to prevent him from succumbing to this trap.

The danger of giving in to worldly pleasure is very real and besets many, but in the midst of this peril we have some true soldiers who pass up pleasure, money, and earthly glory to work humbly but fervently to fulfill God's purpose in their lives. This cloud of witnesses is all about us if we will just take a closer look to get a glimpse of their true value.

These are our home missionaries and those who strug-

Nitty-Gritty for Ministers' Wives

gle to pastor very small churches year after year, disappointment after disappointment, with very little, if any, financial assistance. They live where seldom is heard an *encouraging* word. A few churches don't grow because of lack of prayer and effort, but they are in the small minority. The overwhelming majority of pastors of small churches sincerely and diligently work with all their heart, mind, and soul. Most of these couples manage without outside assistance. The pastor finds secular employment while he tries to raise up a church and often the wife feels it necessary to work also. They may find a small place to rent, and he may preach with only his wife and children present at first.

The Lord is definitely with them, but often no one could prove it by the way they feel. Yet they faithfully have services week after heart-rending week. They knock doors alone, raise money alone, and have services alone. Many times they feel that they are butting their head against a brick wall until they win a few members to help them along. But not all new converts turn out to be all they hope for; some are of very little help for a very long time, if ever. Often these laborers are many miles from the fellowship of friends and family. They need the encouragement of conferences but often cannot afford to go. If they do manage to go, they may not be as nicely dressed because their money must be spent to pay for church rent, utilities, song books, benches, roof repair, and so on instead of new clothes for the family. They must skip the expensive restaurants and drive until they find a McDonalds.

Some people will sympathize and encourage them for a few years, but if their field is particularly hard—full of

A Cloud of Witnesses

rocks, boulders, and poor soil—and the church remains small, then sympathy and encouragement become harder to find. Some will look at them as if something must be wrong with them because their church isn't growing. How difficult it must be to face those condescending looks! They will try every program and every method that they hear is working so wonderfully somewhere else, but often they will have very little results. Their hearts leap every time a visitor comes in, and they certainly would not dream of overlooking them or being unfriendly. They will sometimes gain four and lose five, as one of their families leaves town in search of employment. Usually it is their best workers. Just when the neighboring pastor is having a great influx, the couple they have the most hope for backslides.

Sometimes it takes years and years to build a congregation. If the town is very small with a very transient population, as in some small military or agricultural towns, the church may never be large although many souls find salvation in its humble altars. To say that the faith of those workers will be severely tried, as well as their patience, is an understatement.

How absolutely priceless is a wife in such a situation who is willing to work, to endure bitter hardships, to go without the many nice things she would love to have, to pray when it seems the Lord is a million miles away (or at least over in the next town blessing the church there), and to trust Him despite the evil doubts Satan whispers in her ear—saying that Jesus does not love her and that she has failed Him miserably or else she would not be in the midst of such hardships! What a jewel is she to keep marching and to hold her head up when it wants to hang

Nitty-Gritty for Ministers' Wives

down! In spite of Satan's lies and the seeming lack of fruit, she will remain confident that this barren wilderness is indeed the will of God for her at this time. Her value is beyond estimation, but how many mortals are aware of her? But Jesus knows her and must surely point her out to the angels as one of His choice gems.

One of God's jewels that I am privileged to know personally is Sister Patricia Burgess. Although she and Brother Burgess successfully pastored other churches, they once labored with much prayer and fasting in a town in Nevada, doing everything and trying every program that they felt might bring results. She told me that once, while passing out tracts which were rudely rejected, she broke down and cried in the street. They were there for three years and underwent many hardships, including much physical pain as a result of a car accident, yet they never gained a single soul. Though they had offers of churches in other cities, they worked in that city faithfully until the Lord told Brother Burgess that it was time to move. However, the trials and testing that she went through during that time helped to prepare and strengthen her to be a fine missionary to Argentina and Paraguay, where she loyally and happily followed her husband to work for the Lord.

Many times the only understanding that pastors of small churches receive, if any, is from relatives or close friends, for not many others recognize them or can quite remember their names. They truly rejoice when another one hundred souls are added to another church that was already very large, but they can't help but grieve a little because they still only have ten members and three of these are troublemakers. What faith it takes to live under

A Cloud of Witnesses

such circumstances with little or no help and with seemingly no admiration or gratitude from anyone! God alone knows the extent of their devotion, sacrifice, and trials. They have been through the fire and could write a book about the million varieties of flames. I am glad that God will not judge us by what appears to be a success or failure to mankind but by what He knows about the effort, prayer, sweat, worry, love, faithfulness, and sincerity with which we serve Him.

We met many such dedicated couples on deputation. Many were very sweet and very apologetic for not being able to do more, but they need not feel that way. I was so proud of them that my heart would nearly burst when I saw their devotion to the Lord. My, how I love them!

It is not easy to continue to pastor a small church and suffer the many embarrassments that seem to come when you don't grow as quickly as Pastor A in section B. Not everyone is willing to endure such a life when it calls for living frugally year after year and remaining virtually unknown with no recognition for one's labor. Unfortunately, a few become bitter and suspicious about others who are experiencing quick growth, or they begin to practice poor ministerial ethics in order to persuade people to attend their church. But, again, these are in the minority; most pastors work and live in such a way that they will be able to face the Lord without fear or shame as they give an account of their ministry.

Some of the most remarkable pastors and pastors' wives are those who work, suffer, and endure for many, many years to establish a church as a good-sized congregation and then leave it to begin again from scratch in some other city or state. No doubt it hurts them to leave and

Nitty-Gritty for Ministers' Wives

take up those deep roots, especially knowing what they will probably face for several more years, but when Jesus says, "Go!" they surrender their own will and obey Him. What jewels they must be in the hands of the Lord, for obeying Him and keeping a good spirit is more important to them than establishing a big name for themselves. It would be so much easier to stay at this site of their long-fought-for victory, but they submit to His will and go to another city to begin all over again. This act does not take brilliant intelligence, fantastic talent, or superhuman ability. What it does require is a deep dedication, all-consuming love for the Lord, and a burden for the lost. I am so proud of them and willingly take my hat off to them. You see, they are my brothers and sisters.

In the book *Heirs Together* compiled by Marvelle Dees, I found another cloud of witnesses. These ladies share our precious faith, and I'm sure not one of them claims to have attained perfection. They are real-life woman who are sincere with the Lord and have learned through countless difficulties, heartaches, disappointments, poverty, mistakes, defeats, and at times sheer drudgery to trust in the Lord with all their heart in spite of what they have to face. They too have mopped floors, washed dirty dishes, cooked countless meals, changed dirty diapers, and lived with husbands who at times drove them up the wall. These are women who are no more superhuman than you or I. They have not flitted easily from one success to another but have learned by experience how to live through trials and adversity. They know what it takes to be a good minister's wife and mother because they have been there.

Their advice is not glib, superficial, or impossible to

A Cloud of Witnesses

implement. They don't confess all of their mistakes; they just tell what they have learned as a result of making them. It is not easy to live as they advise, but it can be done by all who will make up their mind that they can and will be the best Christian wife and mother possible with the help of the Lord. This won't come easily for us, nor was it for them. They did it, however, and those living are still doing it. So can we.

Let me share a few tidbits from this book until you can read it or reread it for yourself and possibly underline the parts you need to remember most.

Sister Nellie Cook wrote, "We must realize that as ministers' wives we are not immune to the heartaches of life such as severe sickness, death, and even unsaved children." Many times because of financial difficulties Sister Cook had to trust God for the very food she ate. She also says, "For a period of fourteen years while we had young children (five) at home, I never attended a conference. However, I made certain that my husband attended, saw him off cheerfully, and kept the home fires burning in his absence. While he was away, I attended church regularly with the children, helped to keep the services going, and welcomed him home with open arms when his trip was over. I knew that in order to face the duties of his ministry my husband needed the strength these conferences provided." Difficult for her? You know it was!

Sister Bessie Pugh and her husband evangelized for a year or so with the bus and train as their only means of transportation. She says, "Not having a car was not the worst thing that ever happened to us; in fact, I think it might have been good for us." She still has the same great spirit and attitude toward the work of the Lord.

Sister Catherine Chambers, the wife of our former general superintendent, freely admits that in their early years of ministry it took tongues and interpretation to make her willing to leave a large city and go with her husband to pastor in a small mining town in Pennsylvania. Concerning this experience she says, "The Lord had confirmed my husband's calling and told me that I must be willing to go wherever He called. It was my husband that God had called and as his wife and helpmate, I too must be willing to obey God's call. I have tried through the years to always remember this message and to be willing to go wherever the Lord led my husband. To do otherwise would have been detrimental to the work of the Lord and unfair to the man I had promised to love, honor, and obey till death us do part."

Sister Minnie Wise's husband pastored for many years and suffered many hardships. She told of her husband in later years, "He was so concerned in seeing others saved that he felt he had neglected his own family to a great extent." This feeling is shared by a great many ministers today, but more and more ministers are learning the importance of ministering to their own households. Many are taking Mondays to spend just with the family—I wish it had always been done.

After pastoring for many years, her husband resigned their church and began to evangelize. "I always did my best not to prove a burden to the lady of the house where we were staying. Despite the fact that for almost all this period of time Brother Wise was severely crippled, I was still able to care for him and assist with the housework wherever we were staying. I drove the car when we

A Cloud of Witnesses

traveled. . . . After Brother Wise resigned as superintendent because of his health, we traveled three more years in Louisiana and other states, with Brother Wise preaching and teaching the Bible. During this time it was necessary that I bathe and dress him, although I did not let the public know my burden. I faced it with a smile, as I appreciated my husband's faithfulness in going like he did as long as he could. Many times he would tell me, 'Mother, I feel like I made a failure tonight,' but I assured him he hadn't."

And I can assure you that although she faced her tasks with a smile, there were many times she smiled when she certainly did not *feel* like smiling. But she knew her job was to encourage and uplift others and that a long-faced, complaining MW will only drag others down. So she kept her difficulties and tears private and kept giving smiles to those she was called to help.

Sister Margie Becton says, "I wouldn't want to deceive you, dear, in telling you that every phase of our lives ends with 'and they lived happily ever after.' Far from it. Some experiences end 'and they suffered for the Lord' or 'the burdens of life were *nearly* more than they could bear,' or 'tragedy after tragedy came their way.' . . . Others have known great sorrow, but their sorrow was kept silent, all because God's grace was sufficient for them." And yet to see Sister Becton's beautiful, beaming smile no one would think she knows anything of suffering and sorrow. She also adds, "A daily prayer life is a must. . . . The secret closet of prayer is the place God looks for those He would choose to reward openly."

Each of the ladies in the book have some real diamonds to share, but I can only mention a few here. They lived their experiences one day at a time, dish by dish, heartache by heartache, joy by joy. Their advice is accurate and real because they are so real. The main thing we should remember is that they are all normal women who married men whom God called to preach. Each of them had to learn to be faithful to the Lord and to be a good minister's wife through much effort, endurance, tears, and prayers. In spite of their shortcomings and mistakes, their own dedication and sincerity before God helped them to overcome their many and various obstacles. They were not victorious because they were born saints. And most, if not all, would refuse to change places with anyone else in the world, for, as with anyone who serves the Lord, the good times more than make up for the bad times.

The Lord can and will do the same for you if you will allow Him to work through you as He sees fit to accomplish the purpose for which he has called you. As Sister Dora Guidroz put it, "Do not question the place, the time, or the reason; only be willing to put God first and always in your heart say, 'Yes, God.'"

Let's be honest: there are no superstars among us, and no one can ever get much accomplished for Jesus while lying in a bed of roses. We are all just people—each working, struggling, rejoicing, laughing, crying, and marching forward. We are each full of imperfections, but we blend together to make a perfect bride for Him.

The "witnesses" I have mentioned in this chapter; the many wives I was privileged to work among in California who influenced me, guided me, and strengthened my weak knees with their fine counsel and sweet friendship, especially Sister Ongilee Ogden; the wives I have met and observed on deputation; and the missionary wives have all had many ups and downs. Each has her share of critics, and no doubt each has made her share of mistakes, but each has the goal of doing her best and someday meeting the Lord in peace. I want to be faithful and join them on that great morning.

As one anonymous home missionary states, "I am sure God could have chosen better material to work with than I, but He could never have chosen anyone more willing to try."

That is all He asks!

See why I love my fellow ministers' wives and am so proud of them? I especially love the Lord who called and chose them, and I am very happy that to this great group of sisters He has also chosen to add *you.*

May you be blessed and may you *be* a blessing is my prayer in Jesus' name.